THE CHRONICLES OF
WOMEN IN WHITE COATS

Managing Editor: Amber Robins, MD, MBA

Copy Editor: Karen Williams

Book Cover: Creatif Design Studio

Published by A. Robins Nest, LLC

ISBN: 978-1987634662

Belle
Listen to the
voice w/in
AND Always Dream Big
Kendra Segura

THE CHRONICLES OF
WOMEN IN WHITE COATS

Belle,
I hope this inspires you!.
Donnelly Johny MD

Belle,
Keep walking in life
with faith.

A.
ROBINS
NEST
MEDIA

For my Family and to those who Dare to Dream

CONTENTS

INTRODUCTION

LATASHA S. SELIBY, MD

When I was young girl I wanted to be Clair Huxtable. The beautiful, witty, intelligent, confident, take charge queen mother of the Huxtable household from the Cosby Show. She was a fantastic wife to her physician husband Heathcliff (also known as Cliff), an amazing mother of five, and a successful attorney. Who could blame me for wanting to be her, better yet what young, black girl born in the eighties didn't want to be her.

In the 5th grade we did a research project on careers and salaries, and I learned that female attorneys made less than their male counterparts; at which point I decided that I would rather be Clair with Heathcliff's job; my report did not cover any such discrepancy in physicians' pay. I'd figured if Clair made less then Cliff had to make more. So medical doctor I would be, no matter the cost.

That yearning stuck with me no matter how hard I tried to shake it, and I tried to shake it because I later learned the path to medicine was an arduous one. This desire to practice medicine is one I share with my sister physicians in *The Chronicles of Women in White Coats*. The day we committed ourselves to our respective journeys into medicine, we in turn pledged ourselves to lives of repeated mental assessments and reassessments of our dreams much like the childhood "Clair Huxtable vision" I sacrificed.

As physicians, we constantly must weigh our dreams with sacrifices and balance titles and the roles of our daily lives while battling to gain the same respect as our male counterparts in a world that has been socialized to *not* envision us when they hear the title doctor.

Through the pages of *The Chronicles of Women in White Coats* you will experience our stories. You will walk in our shoes, Danscos versus stilettos depending on the day, through the dimly lit hospital hallways or busy medical offices corridors. These were places where one would think the practice of medicine would be straightforward, yet the art of medicine against the backdrop of implicit bias never fails to elicit moments of the aforementioned assessment and reassessment of thoughts and experiences.

The authors of this book are fearless in their endeavors and even more powerful in their willingness to let you into their inner conflicts, the realization of their dreams, and the epiphanies that clarify the visions they have for both themselves and the communities they serve.

The glimpse into the minds and hearts of these women who are your sisters, wives, daughters, mothers, friends — and happen to also be your doctors — will surprise you. These stories will not fail to amaze you, make you laugh, and maybe even bring you to tears. In doing so, we hope they will allow you to understand the level of commitment to their craft as they walk out this fabulous adventure called life in their rightfully earned - sometimes neatly pressed - white coats.

CODE BLUE

ALEXANDRA PIÑON, MD

"My baby stopped breathing!" the panicked voice echoed across the ward and cut through the hum of voices at the nursing station. "Help!" The beehive of activity at the desk halted; our collective breaths held as every head turned to look at the far side of the large playroom that was the center of the pediatric ward.

My feet started moving involuntarily towards the voice. I looked up from the paper in my hand as I took a step and then started jogging. I was the resident on call for the pediatric ward that afternoon, and I had been standing at the nurses' station talking to the residents from the day shift to learn about the patients that would be under my care that evening. We hadn't yet finished the sign out process, and we hadn't talked about that room. I didn't know this baby. Rushing into that room I was running into the unknown.

The dull weight of anxiety throbbed in my chest as I saw a mother standing helplessly in the doorway of a patient room with tears streaming down her face. She was holding up a small, pale infant in both hands. The infant's face was dusky, her mouth slack, and her arms and legs dangled uselessly as her mother held her up to us. I don't recall saying it, but my voice projected clear and loud across the ward to call a code blue. On some level I stepped outside myself, watching the events that would unfold.

I hadn't run a code before. It was something that terrified me, but I knew it would happen at some point. I had passed the necessary training to participate in a code, but thankfully critical events such as this one were relatively rare in pediatrics. Would I remember all the steps to evaluating and treating my patient? Would I freeze or be paralyzed by anxiety and doubt? I had carefully memorized the algorithms and practiced in my mind what I would do in just this situation, but would the scenarios I had memorized translate into competence in an emergency?

The limp infant just filled my cupped hands as I carried her into the patient room and laid her on her crib mattress. Pieces of information fluttered about my mind, small scraps of paper swirling in the hurricane of my thoughts, disordered and useless. I was vaguely aware of the clinical staff around me as they removed the canopy from the hospital crib giving us better access to the bed. I half noticed that a crash cart was being wheeled into the room.

"Are you ok?" I asked the small child, rubbing her back, rubbing her sternum, trying to elicit a response. The first step of a code. There was no cry; her tiny face didn't grimace in response to the rubbing on her chest. There was no movement; there was no breath. And then I felt a heartbeat. Under my hand the tiny impulse of her heart pressed up against my fingertips. She was in there; a small little life. It seemed as if she had reached up and grabbed my fingers clinging to them. That sensation overwhelmed my senses; it was stronger than the sobs of her mother in the corner of the patient room, louder than the intercom blaring a code blue announcement, and even louder than the voices around me wheeling the crash cart, dismantling the crib, and gathering supplies. I felt it tapping between the toothpick contours of her ribs, and that gentle nudge had the effect of an electric shock. My mind cleared. The scraps of paper jumbled in my thoughts came together, and I could see the steps of a code. I could see what to do next. My training kicked in, and I took a deep breath and proceeded. Count the pulse. Look at your watch and count the pulse. I counted for 10 seconds. "Her heart rate is 100," I said to the team. "She's not breathing. We need to give breaths. Where is the mask?"

As I counted that tiny heart beat, a dance was unfolding around me. A nurse placed an oxygen sensor on the baby's toe which would count her heart rate and measure her oxygen saturation on the monitor. Another nurse was preparing to place an IV so we could give medications if they were needed. Someone else handed me a self-inflating bag with a mask so we could start to give breaths. "Who is timing?" I asked as I placed the mask over her nose and mouth. A voice came from behind me, "I am," as I carefully positioned her head. I checked her mouth and tongue and noted the sour smell of old milk, but her airway was clear. She must have refluxed; I thought to myself.

The mask fit easily over her nose and mouth; her diminutive size giving the impression that I had placed it on a baby doll. I pressed the plastic bag pushing air into those fragile lungs. The air entered easily, and her chest expanded. A nurse listened with her stethoscope and nodded to me that the air was moving in her lungs as it should. The quiet of the room was broken only by the mechanic pulse on the heart rate monitor, but a silent roar of will surged through the charged air. It was a scream of hope that emanated from each of us, begging her to breathe. Another push on the bag, another rise of her chest, and I sent another prayer riding on oxygen into her body, begging a response.

"Will she breathe again?" I asked myself. "Will her heart slow and stop?" The thought came unbidden such as a nightmare creeping out of the shadows in my mind. "Can I save her, or is she going to be torn away from us?" And then the questions every young doctor must ask themselves, "Am I doing this right; have I forgotten anything? Am I going to fail this patient, this family?" The Hippocratic oath tells us to first do no harm. As physicians we cannot always heal or cure although this is the goal, but we can provide solace, ease pain, and mitigate disease. Above all things we must strive to never, either by action or omission, make something worse. At some point every physician will ask themselves if they are causing harm instead of good, even with the best of intentions. At that moment, as a junior doctor awaiting the arrival of a more experienced physician to give guidance, I struggled to find assurance that I was doing the right thing.

Another breath delivered with shaky fingers as doubt coursed through my veins. "Please breathe," I whispered through gritted teeth. Did I see her fingers move? Another breath, "please breathe," I whispered again. The silence of the room seemed heavier, oppressive. Another breath, and suddenly her tiny face twisted into a grimace, her arms startled and raised in the air, and an ear-piercing wail cut through the heavy blanket of anticipation that had shrouded the room. The monotonous beep of the heart rate monitor sped up as her pulse quickened. I placed the mask to the side and took a deep breath myself, unaware that I had been holding it even as I had been begging her to breathe.

A tear of relief wandered down my cheek, and the weight of a hand was placed on my shoulder. I looked up into the face of my attending physician. When had she gotten there? "Well done," she said.

The crowd in the room started to move. Preparations were made to move the baby to a higher level of care for observation. I talked to her mother regarding what had happened and the plan to transfer her to the ICU for ongoing care. The team that managed the code met in the conference room of the ward to review what had happened and what needed to be done better. These were preparations we, as providers, could make to give more effective care the next time. I listened intently, provided my observations, and accepted feedback as we discussed the code.

That night once the the ward was quiet, I reflected on the events of the evening. All my patients settled for the night, my rounds for the evening were complete, and I waited for my pager to alert me to my next task. I reflected on what would have happened if I had frozen and not remembered the steps of resuscitation, or if I had proceeded with the code but done them incorrectly.

I was starting to learn that practicing medicine is a balance of risk and benefits; a constant decision-making process. Early in my career each choice I made plagued me with insecurity. I hoped then that someday I would reach a point when my knowledge would overcome any uncertainty. The intervening years have taught me that will not happen, nor do I want it to. It is an integral component to the ongoing development and improvement of any physician. There are infinite variables that must be considered before each step is taken. It never becomes routine or rote; each patient and variable present a different facet of health and disease. I carry the uncertainty that comes from such a complex system as a constant companion. It used to be foreign and terrifying, now it is a familiar adversary clenched in the tight muscles of my shoulders.

We try in medicine to conquer the variables with algorithms, and they are helpful but ultimately should not be the only factor to guide our steps. Time has taught me that in some instances I will be an agile practitioner, making no false steps and gliding smoothly through a patient encounter. Other days I will falter and be thankful for the algorithms that provide direction. In all instances I search for inspiration and an opportunity to treat and heal my patient.

My attending had said, "Well done." And on that day at least, I had done well.

FEAR CAN LEAD TO TRIUMPH

CHARMAINE R. GREGORY, MD

Whenever faced with the prospect of something new, we humans are often challenged to the core. The thing that we tend to forget is that what challenges us, usually leads to the greatest personal growth. Think about how you felt when you tried to ride a bicycle for the very first time. This is a universal shared experience that manifests the innate fear of the unknown. In fact, I can vividly recount the first time that I learned to ride a bicycle; skills I later tapped into as a medical student.

It was a hot day like every other on the island of Jamaica where I grew up. I had just gotten a bicycle for my birthday. My father had come over to visit, as he sometimes did since my parents were not married, to help me learn to ride. We practiced in the parking lot outside of our condominium home. When I got on the bike, I was very nervous. What if I fall? What if I crash? These were not the questions that were paramount in my mind in that moment however. I was more nervous because I was being watched and was afraid that I would not be able to do it. The trepidation that I felt did not deter me from trying. I got on the bike. I extended one leg and made contact with the pedal. I pushed off with my other leg. Then, I made contact with the other pedal. In that instant, I held my breath. It was a very surreal moment and for a split second I felt like I was flying. In an awkward rhythmic dance, one leg bent as the other extended and then again and again. The security of the training wheels was now removed. The reality of being able to do it was what supplanted my fear of embarrassment. That was the day that I rode a two-wheel bicycle. That was the day that I gained the skills that will not be forgotten.

Often, in order to learn and master a skill, it takes deliberate practice. At first we may be afraid of messing up. Initially, we may consider every step extremely carefully, but then we become mindful of the sequence of steps. We begin to do the movement or the process over and over — practice. Before long that process becomes automatic. That first day I had to think about moving those pedals, maintaining balance on those two wheels, and being aware of where I was headed. Now when I ride a bike, the details of the mechanics of riding are not at the fore of my thoughts. In fact, I can talk to my children, listen to music, and be aware of my surroundings while my legs instinctively propel me forward and my cerebellum keeps me upright on the two wheels.

There was a time when I thought that fear was a bad thing. In thinking about the evolution of fear, it serves a very different purpose today than it did for our prehistoric ancestors. For them, fear was life or death. It stimulated the adrenaline rush that allowed for fight or flight when a predator was near. In the day and age when we are not prey for saber tooth tigers, fear's ubiquitous presence has a different utility. It is key to tap into this source of energy and momentum. This is one of the valuable lessons learned as I explored this emotion. Fear will always be present. What we do with fear is really all that matters. There have been many times in my life as an adult when I was afraid. On many of these occasions, my utilization of that fear has evolved tremendously.

In my third year of medical school, I was afforded the opportunity to be a resident at the NIH Howard Hughes Cloister program on the campus of the NIH in Bethesda, Maryland. Participating in this program meant taking the year off from medical school, but this was my opportunity to find out if being a physician scientist was for me, short of another graduate degree. I remember the day that I arrived on the NIH campus. It was August, and the campus was verdant and ripe with opportunity. I remember how excited I felt to be amongst other young minds who were eager to learn and grow. Some of my classmates had clear goals and direction for the year. However, I was not as certain but was open to discovery and the exploration of the available options. It was eye-opening to be involved in this program at a place where the principal investigators had resources and could provide a level of mentorship that was nothing short of stellar.

My tenure at the NIH was in the lab of distinguished diabetes researcher, Marc Reitman, MD, PhD. This was the first time that I felt the true intensity of the impostor syndrome. I felt like my brilliance was not on the same level as those around me. I feared that I would fail. The funny thing about that though was I was not crippled by my fears. Instead, I was oblivious to them. I did not think deeply about how these items would potentially affect my outcome. Instead, I just gave it my best. Spending that year in the program afforded me some amazing experiences and opportunities. Being in the lab, working closely with the physician scientist, and seeing the possibility of translational research was nothing short of spectacular. However, as amazing as it was, I knew that was not the path for me.

The second time that I felt intense fear was the first day of my emergency medicine internship. Here I was, a freshly minted doctor, faced with the responsibility of actually caring for patients on my own. On the first day, during the first week, in the first month every order that I wrote and every decision that I made had an undertone of fear. As the days progressed, and the number of patients seen increased, my fear diminished. I had different challenges beyond the medical decision-making that were actually unforeseen. You see at age 10 or 11, I looked like I was about 16 or 17, but then as I progressed to my 20's, that youthful appearance seemed to be suspended in time. This was a challenge because I had to convince my patients that I was actually old enough to make medical decisions about their care. Of course, wearing my hair in a youthful style did not improve the perception. I discovered ways to compensate for this; for example, I would wear my white coat at all times.

The interesting thing about that particular problem is that it took on a whole different face once I became an attending. Now I wear the white coat not only because of my face but also because of my gender. It was not out of the question that I would be mistaken for the nurse instead of the doctor. I started my career wearing my white coat at all times and that has been a habit that has stayed with me.

The fear I felt as an intern was eventually mitigated by hours of practice, revision after feedback, and numerous patient encounters. I eventually stopped having sweaty palms and palpitations every time I wrote an order for morphine. Of course, with the years following training and the acquisition of thousands of patient encounters, some of these base fears have been superseded. Again, as an intern I felt the fear but did my job anyway. I failed forward on numerous occasions and pressed on. Training was grueling in the era of 22 twelve-hour shifts in a month and 100+ hours a week on the surgical service before the implementation of regulated work hours. My tenure was just as the eighty work hour weekly limit was being implemented so I got to see the coin on both sides.

The third time I was afraid was when I was unsuccessful in passing my recertification board exam by missing the mark by one point. This was a dark time for me. There I was in my last eligible year of certification, distracted by life and all its accoutrements, staring at the word FAIL on the white sheet of paper topped with the insignia of the American Board of Emergency Medicine in light pine green. I was in total disbelief. How could this have happened? I spent so much time studying. What does this failure mean for my job and my career? Was this the end? My family had grown financially dependent on the income that practicing emergency medicine provided. The fear that riddled me was tremendous. I honestly felt like my world was caving in on me. Fear, there it was again, omnipresent. I had not expected or even truly feared actual failure. But yet, here it was staring me audaciously in the face, gripping my face in its frigid hands, and daring me to take action.

Don't get me wrong, there was at least a day or two during which I wallowed deeply in self pity chased with a dollop of depression. After that brief catharsis, it was time to devise a game plan of action. So, despite being very afraid of what was to become of me and my family's future, I chose to make some phone calls and come up with a battle plan. The first call was to my medical director who was very encouraging and compassionate. It was in these moments that I realized that facing this fear and feeling this particular pain ensured that my comeback story would be a great one. The fear that I felt became the catalyst for action and the motivation to press on even when I did not feel like it. No single point could characterize the care that I provide my patients on a nightly basis. No single point defines me as a physician.

This hardship rocked me to the core. My true self was revealed. My internal fabric turned out to be composed of resilience and grit. I wiped away my tears and drafted a plan of action. My husband was a huge support during this time and is the reason why I can write about this now. We sat down and mapped out my plan. Starting with the test date, we reverse engineered how many hours and how many questions I would need to complete in order to not only pass but crush the exam. It was clearly the long game, and my plan spanned nine months. Please understand that I was still afraid, but I used that fear to stoke the fire inside myself instead of allowing it to cripple me. I fell forward; I failed forward.

The exam day arrived, and my vibe was as cool as a cucumber. That morning I arrived at the testing center; I was amped with thoughts of warrior type victory. There may or may not have been some repeated viewing of my favorite motivational YouTube videos to spark a winner's mindset. As I completed question after question (and there were hundreds), my mindset was that of triumph, and my view of the test was that of gamesmanship. To be honest, I was actually having fun taking a standardized test which, if you know me, is unheard of. How is that possible? It was possible because I rerouted my fear and transformed it into positive energy that obliterated the option of not being successful. Don't get me wrong, the test was challenging as is expected from a specialty board exam, but I was ready. My game face was on, and my soul was happy to take on the challenge. The fear I felt when I read that very negative four letter word on the white sheet of paper topped with the insignia of the

American Board of Emergency Physicians in light pine green was now a catalyst for change. Just a few short months after I walked out of the testing center, with the midday sunlight beaming on my face feeling accomplished, another four letter word greeted me – PASS. Yes! I had fallen on my face, but I did not let fear keep me down on the ground. Instead, I got up, dusted my shoulders off, kept my head up, put in the work, and crushed the exam that had previously slain me!

So, these are just three examples of my jaunts with fear, and it is clear to me now that fear is a litmus test for me. Every time that I have been afraid, had that pit deep down in my stomach, and questioned whether I should proceed, there has been a major breakthrough waiting for me on the other side of that fear. My husband and I jest about how I make some of my decisions now. You see, if an opportunity arises, and I feel great fear then I know that is what I must pursue.

An opportunity for leadership at several of the emergency departments that my emergency medicine group staffs arose not too long ago. On paper, I had no practical experience affecting process change or implementing programs, but I applied anyway. The interview process was lengthy and numerous, but it gave me an opportunity to showcase my personal growth. In the end I did not get the position but a delightful side effect occurred. Now the leadership of the group are aware of my interest in administration and the skills that I bring. Now that I am on the radar, suggestions for preparation for the next round of promotions and mentorship are being offered to me. If I had listened to fear and not put my name in the hat, I would be missing out on being included in the discussions of my department's leaders.

Despite not having all the elements in place for many of my life experiences both in and outside of medicine, I used these instances to step out on faith and went for it. I felt the fear and knew that I had to go for it. Life is way too short to stay in my comfort zone. Fear reminds me that taking risks and putting myself out there can yield great reward. My wish for you is that you will feel the fear but do it anyway. You have nothing but treasure on the other side. Be strong. Be brave. Unleash your greatness.

❧ 3 ❧

FOREVER CHANGED

ARCHANA R. SHRESTHA, MD

T here are certain life experiences that leave you forever changed at your core. Becoming a doctor and a parent are two of them. And while it doesn't happen overnight, each one profoundly changes the way you view and approach the world.

First Lesson: Medicine 101

BEING A DOCTOR IS NOT JUST A VOCATION, IT IS SOMETHING that changes your identity. Not only did medicine forever change the way I understood the human body, but it also gave me life experiences that most young adults don't have. Even though I was just 21 years old when I started medical school, training to become a doctor made me mature quickly and made me a part of some of the most raw and life-changing moments in people's lives. As a result, I saw the best of humanity, as well as its dark side.

I saw babies come into this world and take their very first breath; I witnessed people take their last dying breath. I cared for both the victims of horrible child abuse and cancer survivors whose resilience amazed me. I watched people in excruciating pain from severe trauma and others in intense gratitude that they were still alive after a bad accident.

Medicine brought me face to face with people from all walks of life, of all races, ages and socioeconomic status. In my years training, I cared for gang members, prisoners, and homeless people as well as diplomats, senators, and movie actors. I helped care for minute old preemies that were hardly bigger than my hand, to grandmas that were 110 years old.

In the process, I had all sorts of bodily fluids accidentally land on me — everything from saliva, to vomit and blood. In doing physical exams, I had my gloved fingers in every imaginable orifice of the human body and in surgery touched just about every single organ inside of a living human being. To say you are changed by medical training and will never see the body quite the same as you did before starting medical school is an understatement.

Once you are well-versed in the inner workings of the human body, it's hard to go back to the way you used to understand it; the way people outside of medicine understand the body. It is a struggle at first to not use medical jargon with patients. A shoulder blade is now a scapula, and the collarbone is a clavicle. SOB no longer is a curse but forever means shortness of breath. A person with the initials B.M. will always make me giggle inside because to me it now stands for bowel movement.

You also get good at asking questions and wanting to know the exact details of what patients are complaining about because it is only then that you can begin to make a diagnosis and help them. You are "sick to your stomach?" Are you throwing up? Having diarrhea? How many times in the last 24 hours? What color was the vomit? Was there any blood in it? How many times a day are you having diarrhea? Did you eat something that may have gotten you sick or have you traveled anywhere recently?

You develop skill at reading people too, reading between the lines of what people are saying, and knowing when people are not giving you the full story. You get savvy and street smart and can call people's bluff even if you don't say it.

Things that are so obvious to those of us in medicine sometimes are completely novel to patients. That is where the art of medicine comes in, and you start to understand that anatomy, pathology, and pharmacology are one thing, but how you are going to explain it and get your patient to listen to what you have to say is another thing entirely. You start to realize that there are so many different ways to understand the body. While learning these concepts, I longed to explore medicine and healing in a broader way; an adventure that took me around the world.

The World As My Teacher

I BEGAN MY EXPLORATION AFTER MY THIRD YEAR OF medical school traveling to Ecuador to study medical anthropology as a Fulbright fellow. In Ecuador, I observed traditional healers. My medical training had given me a mindset and framework that was not only different from my patients but also different from traditional healers. The shamans, sobaderos (bone setters) and midwives spoke of evil eye, bad air, and hot and cold imbalance. They used medicinal plants to heal as well as rituals and prayer. As a member of the research team, I diligently cataloged the medicinal plants and studied them to better understand their healing properties. The experience taught me that while I had been engrossed in my world of western allopathic medicine, there was another world out there with completely different practices and beliefs with its own frameworks for understanding the human body. The juxtaposition of what I had learned in medical school and the beliefs of traditional healers fascinated me. Was there a bridge between the two? Could some of the medicinal herbs be used in western medicine as well? Could these medicinal plants help the masses?

Fascinated by the cultural differences of practicing medicine in different countries, I delved deeper. In residency, I traveled to India to do a rotation in a large urban hospital and thought about doing international emergency medicine by helping to set up improved emergency medical systems in countries where they had yet to be fully established. India, at the time, had no 911 or Emergency Medical Services system in place. When someone was critically injured or ill, precious minutes were often lost as family members or bystanders struggled to figure out who to call for help and what to do in the moment to help the person in need.

Though I found this an opportunity to change a piece of the world, reality set in. Once I got married, with hopes of becoming a parent one day, I began to wonder how I would travel abroad and leave my family.

I didn't want to work in another country for a month or more and not see my family during that time. That kind of lifestyle was not appealing for me. So I put it aside to perhaps come back to it one day and decided that after more than a decade of college, medical school and residency training this next season in my life was meant to be with my husband and the family that we would one day have.

Becoming a Mom

WHILE IN GENERAL I LOVED BEING AN EMERGENCY

physician, I did not enjoy being a pregnant doctor. I disliked all the discomforts of pregnancy and having to work pregnant in the uncontrolled environment of the ER. I remember being pregnant for the first time as an attending physician working in the emergency room. I had seen so many women come in having miscarriages or with complications after giving birth that I wondered if the same would happen to me.

I couldn't just be a happy and excited pregnant lady. Knowing too much and having seen so many unfortunate cases during my training were now working against me. I worried about all the radiation my unborn baby was being exposed to from the portable x-rays done in our ER, being around violent patients who sometimes attacked the staff, and of course about catching infections from patients.

One day, while I was pregnant and was inserting a chest tube into a patient with a collapsed lung, my glove broke while my finger was inside the patient's chest cavity. I pulled my index finger out to find the patient's blood on my skin. For months I followed up with our occupational health department to make sure I didn't contract any blood-borne illnesses from the patient. Thankfully, neither I nor my baby were affected.

I remember being pregnant when H1N1 influenza hit our community and many patients came into the ER with flu symptoms. I worried I would catch it and become critically ill in the ICU as this was what we were seeing amongst pregnant women who caught this particular strain of influenza. I got my flu vaccine, donned a face mask for much of my shift, and washed my hands frequently; thankfully, all my measures were successful. I managed to avoid catching influenza. Next step: giving birth to my baby boy.

Even though I had seen and been a part of so many births and found delivering babies to be a joyous and rewarding job, going through labor and giving birth myself scared me the first time around. While the vast majority of deliveries went just fine, there were a few rare and exceptional cases where women needed emergency C-sections or where the baby was stillborn. Would the same happen to me? Although I was nervous, I couldn't wait to have my baby and hold him in my arms, and when I did, I was grateful that everything turned out fine.

After the course of 12 hours in labor, I went from being a pregnant woman to a first time mother fumbling with diapers and swaddling while trying to figure out how to breastfeed my newborn. I still remember when the labor nurse said, "Congratulations, Mom! Hold your beautiful baby," and placed my newborn son in my arms for the very first time. I quickly glanced behind me to see if my mother was standing there because the only one I had heard called "Mom" around me was my own mother. Clearly, the nurse must have been referring to her and not me.

As I held my son for the first time and looked into his bright, sparkly eyes, it was then that I fully realized how this little baby boy was our divine gift and responsibility and that life going forward would never be the same. The birth of my first born was also the birth of my role as a mom. Other roles may come and go, but I would forever be mother to my children for the rest of our lives.

I quickly found that becoming a parent forever changes someone much like becoming a doctor does. Unlike medical school, which came with courses, textbooks and lectures, there is no manual on how to be a good parent or how to raise great kids. No matter how many parenting books I read, how many other moms I spoke to, or how many times I babysat other people's children, nothing prepared me completely for being a parent. Every minute of every day with my child needed to be accounted for, and life would never be the same.

With time, my husband and I gained confidence and settled into a routine with our son. I truly loved his baby year: snuggling with him and watching him roll over, crawl, and walk one day just before he turned one year old. I loved listening to him say his first word, Mama, seeing his first tooth finally had come in, and watching him discover the world of new sights, sounds, smells, shapes, and tastes. Through him, as I watched him grow, I was reliving my own childhood.

He was a happy boy -- but like many mothers I wondered if I was doing things right. I would read up on parenting blogs and ask others for advice, but still would sometimes think, "How could the most important job of my life not come with an instruction manual, a course or training?" But, I followed my maternal instincts, showered him with unconditional love and tons of hugs and kisses, read and played with him a lot and, of course, kept a watchful eye on him to always keep him safe.

Again, when it came to safety, especially in the toddler years, my knowledge as an emergency physician of all that could go wrong got the best of me. All the images of little toddlers who had come in injured would pop into my head: burns from hot coffee sitting on a table, lacerations from sharp objects, or fractured bones from falling down the stairs. And then, there were the times kids got into pills or cleaning supplies or choked on marbles or coins.

I admit I was the nervous mom who needed to baby proof every nook and cranny of not only our house but grandma's house too since my son spent a lot of time there. I even got rid of the coffee table altogether replacing it with an ottoman because I had just seen too many toddlers come into the ER with forehead or eyebrow lacerations from bumping their heads on the coffee table corners. I loved my baby so much that I didn't want him to have any of those injuries, and the thought of something happening to him, after all I knew and had seen, was just too much. The look of sadness and remorse on the parent's face whenever accidents like these happened was heartbreaking. I didn't want that same feeling and did as much as I could to avoid it.

As my son grew up healthy, and thankfully without any major illnesses or injuries, I realized that my perception had been clouded to some degree. Some of the worry I experienced was similar to many first-time parents, but it was perhaps heightened by what I had seen at work. In the ER we see all the bad accidents, injuries and illnesses. We see all the extreme things that can happen, but of course they don't happen often when the proper precautions are taken.

I am happy to say that during my second pregnancy and in raising my second child, I was less worried and realized that just because an injury or illness happened to one of my pediatric patients didn't mean it was going to happen to my own children.

Being a mom who is also a doctor had some perks too. I didn't have to call the pediatrician very often since I usually could diagnose my children's illnesses myself. I was a pro at dosing over the counter medicines. I also knew whether my kids' cuts needed stitches or their injured wrist or ankle needed x-rays. Not to mention, all the other moms at play groups wanted to be my friend because who doesn't want to have a doctor friend that they can dial up to ask a quick question about their child?

Becoming a mother made me a better doctor because, as a mom, I could truly relate to other parents and the concerns that were going through their minds when they brought their child to us. Also, having kids of my own allowed me to understand the growth and development of children and gave me things to chat about with my littlest patients. I would talk to my pediatric patients about sports, their favorite ice cream flavors, and the latest Disney Junior cartoon characters. I would also tell them about my own kids and their favorite things and when they realized that I was a mom, they seemed more at ease. Then, I would enjoy giving them stickers at the end of their visit and seeing their faces light up when they saw the surprise.

When I would come home from work, my own children would ask if I'd seen any kids that day and why they had come to the hospital. My kids have been fascinated by my work and often proudly tell their friends, "My mommy is a doctor."

The Woman I Am Today

AS THE YEARS HAVE GONE BY, BEING A DOCTOR AND A parent have become the essence of who I am. I live and breathe the two. I can wake from my sleep and instinctively know how to do either one. Becoming an emergency physician and experiencing medicine around the world took eight dedicated years of intense and intentional study and practice while becoming a parent happened more instinctively and with lots of on the job training. While both have forever changed me, they have made me better and taken me to some of the most sacred and intimate places in my patients' lives as well as my own family life. I have the privilege and joy of being a mother to my two wonderful children and also of serving my patients in their moments of need. Sometimes people ask me how I juggle it all, being a doctor and a mom while engaging in many other roles as well, but it is just who I am and who I have become over time: my training and experiences molding and shaping me into the mother, doctor and woman I am today.

❧ 4 ❧

BOUNDARIES

ALEXANDRA PIÑON, MD

I struggled to maintain my composure, watching in the rear-view mirror, as the police officer approached my car. My pounding heart ached, straining against the too tight walls of my chest, and my eyes stung with unshed tears. I cleared my throat and tried to swallow the golf ball of fear that had lodged there. I was aware I had been speeding. I looked down at the scrub pants and t-shirt I had put on that morning; it was a t-shirt from a health fair my medical school had hosted that year. I had thrown on the ensemble as I ran out the door that morning to take a test. The day was going so differently from the one I had envisioned. The officer tapped on my window, and I rolled it down. The humid Florida air rolled in as I looked up into the officer's sunglass obscured face.

"In a rush to see Mickey Mouse?" he asked with a smirk.

The tears came; I wish I had been going to see Mickey Mouse. My grandfather was lying in a hospital in Orlando dying. I had been driving on the highway between Miami and Orlando, my speed determined by my anxiety, to see him before he passed. Taking a wavering breath, I prepared to explain the situation to the officer, but my words betrayed me and jumped staccato between sobs. "My grandfather is in the hospital; I'm going to see him."

The officer was taken aback by the raw emotion of my response. He stuttered, "Ahh. Uh. Okay, well, you need to slow down. Follow the speed limit, and uh...drive safely. Don't let me catch you speeding again." I nodded my assent, unable to try to talk further as the tears dripped off my chin. He turned to walk back to his patrol car with the crunching of his boots on the gravel announcing his departure. I took several deep breaths and gripped the steering wheel to calm down before pulling out into traffic again. I started out carefully watching my speed.

During the drive my thoughts wandered through memories of Granddaddy. My sister and I would spend summers at his and my grandmother's house. He had been an elementary school principal and teacher. He had retired long before those lazy, warm, summer afternoons we spent exploring the parks and beaches in Tampa, but even in his retirement he was an inveterate educator. I remembered him interrupting our television shows to discuss excerpts on famous artists from an encyclopedia or identifying species of trees and foliage when we walked through the parks. I remembered fishing with him. I remembered his soft-spoken voice, the twinkle in his eye when he was suggesting something mischievous, and his manners that never failed. He was polite and kind to everyone. I remember that he deferred to my grandmother, the love of his life, in nearly all things. He was the gentleman's gentleman. As each memory swam to the surface of my thoughts, the weight of my foot increased, and it wasn't long before the speedometer crept above the limit. I arrived at the hospital in record time.

My mother met me at the hospital that afternoon. The strain of the situation with my grandfather's worsening health showed on her face. Her eyes usually smiled, just like his always did, but that day fear and exhaustion dampened their shine. As we traversed the lobby and hallways towards Granddaddy's hospital room, we discussed his declining health. The management of his congestive heart failure and emphysema had required frequent admissions to the hospital. This admission followed the previous by only 24 hours as his breathing became increasingly labored. Seven days had passed, and his condition had become complicated by an infection, but the source was not yet identified; his doctors were considering pneumonia or possibly his pacemaker leads. Despite treatment with antibiotics he had been getting worse, and the blood culture results showed resistant bacteria called MRSA.

Although he had always needed intermittent assistance with his breathing, his oxygen levels were worsening, and his doctors were having trouble maintaining them. His sleep was poor, and he would become agitated and cry "help me" in the night. Fluid had started to collect around his lungs. A nasal cannula puffed a thin trail of oxygen into his nose, but he couldn't tolerate more oxygen despite his need for it. Given his tenuous status the decision was made not to remove the fluid from around his lungs because it would be an invasive and painful procedure. Instead, my mother made the heart wrenching decision to provide comfort measures while the infection raged and nature ran its course.

The morning my mother telephoned me, his white blood cell count was fifty thousand, more than 5 times the normal level signifying that his infection was getting worse, and it had been increasing over the last week. The phone call I received that morning was a last call; it was time to say goodbye.

I had been surprised by my mother's call that morning. When the phone rang, I was walking happily out of a medical school exam, feeling optimistic that it had gone well and pleased by its completion. I knew Granddaddy had been sick, but the gravity of the situation had escaped me. I was a fourth-year medical student and fully absorbed by the hectic demands of exams, clinical rotations, and planning for residency. Just the week before, I had matched to a pediatrics program at the Naval Hospital in San Diego. The first stage of my training was nearly complete; I stood poised to graduate in a couple of months and acquire the title of doctor. How much I thought I knew then! Still, the feeling of uncertainty as I entered my grandfather's hospital room was inescapable. I had no training on how to be a patient or the family member of a patient. I had no idea how to address death. I sought shelter in facts and objective data – lab results, clinical plans, medications. It is always easier to march forward with a concrete plan knowing what to do rather than wondering and watching events unfold.

My sister, who lived closer than I did, had been more present throughout the process and had helped in my grandfather's care. She was there when I walked into the hospital room, crooning soothingly to his confusion and agitation. My mother jumped into action on arrival as well, adjusting his nasal cannula.

I felt like a stranger in the room — my position in the family unfamiliar. I had spent so much energy learning to be a physician, but now I was out of my element. I greeted my sister and gave my grandfather an awkward hug. I tried to speak slowly and enunciate as I asked how he felt. My words clunked dull to the floor unanswered, ignored either due to his hearing loss or his mental status. The smell of a hospital room shouldn't have bothered me, but it did that day. It smelled like stale air and illness masked with an antiseptic and served to augment the chasm of difference I felt between myself and my family.

We passed the time that afternoon. I chatted with my

sister and tried to catch up on the events of her life. We took turns soothing Granddaddy and helping with oxygen and blankets. We begged him to take any kind of food, but his energy seemed more focused on the rattled breaths he forced in and out of his body. We waited.

I read my grandfather's medical chart, deciphering the jagged handwriting of his doctors and trying to piece together the jigsaw puzzle of his care, searching for a plan or clue that would lend hope to his outcome. I felt so helpless, I prayed his antibiotics would suddenly start to work, and he would improve. My Uncle Gerry arrived that evening. My mother had called him when she called me.

The next morning my grandfather was due for a blood draw to check his white blood cell count again. It seemed so important to me that his blood test was done. All of us were attending to the passage of time and Mother Nature's will, but that test, it seemed to me, would be a marker in the roadmap of his health; a compass needle to show us due north. Granddaddy didn't want it. Entirely lucid, he refused, angrily yanking his arm away from the phlebotomist. I held him. It only took a slight effort to hold his arm still as the glistening edge of a needle was introduced into his vein. As his dark blood sluggishly traveled the plastic tubing, he met my eyes. His faded eyes were fierce, and his glare pierced through the blanket of the unfamiliarity I had felt since my arrival and stabbed at my heart. He was so angry. He did not speak a word. I don't know if he was too sick to yell at me or if his enduring politeness and civility made him hold his tongue. I don't know if he was only mad at me, or if I was the recipient of his anger at doctors, nurses, hospitals, pain, and his own failing body.

Once the blood draw was done, I released his arm and stepped back, unsure and shaken. I wanted to escape that fury, and I was overwhelmed with the feeling that I had inflicted something on him that should not have happened. I attempted to focus on the necessity of the test results to track my grandfather's treatment, trying to assuage the uneasiness his glare had incited. The uneasiness followed me that morning as we tended to him. It followed me when my mother and I left the hospital for a short while to run an errand, leaving my sister and uncle to tend to Granddaddy. It nagged at me when the phone rang to tell us of his passing.

My grandfather died that afternoon.

A thunderbolt of realization tore through me. He had known it was time. He knew that stupid blood draw would do nothing to help his doctors or further his care. It was just another source of pain, the last straw on top of a haystack of medical insults that were attempts to slow his progression to undefeatable death. I held his arm to facilitate his medical care; the care he should have had a right to refuse. In holding him still for that last lab test, I had sided with the health care machine that had progressively dehumanized him. It was a betrayal; I had seen the accusation clearly in his eyes, and the guilt of it dropped heavy into my heart like a stone.

That day I did not understand that my responsibility was only to be his granddaughter. I should have advocated for him. I did not know how to reconcile my medical training with my obligations as a family member. It continues to be a challenge, and as such, I avoid treating family members as much as possible. There are so many other doctors out there, but I am a unique component of my family — my children's only mother, my husband's only wife. It is seductive to think that being a doctor is tantamount to all things, but it is cheap and plastic compared to the warmth of relationships that are woven through years of life and companionship.

It was post mortem, but my grandfather gave me the most profound lesson that day. He taught me that people must always come first. Behind every diagnosis is a breathing, autonomous person with wants and desires and feelings. I am a doctor, and a significant component of my job requires objectivity. It requires performing tests and prescribing medicines, making plans and directing care. Objectivity is what enables health care providers to do their job without being washed away by the enormity of the human experience comprised by fear and pain and want. Without it we would be an exposed nerve — raw and miserable. Objectivity creates a boundary and offers protection. It is dangerous; however, to let those boundaries become too strong or too thick because that is when patients cease to be people, and physicians cease to be healers. Granddaddy showed me a window through that wall, and as long as I remember to keep it open, I am bathed in the warmth of humanity and blessed by the people I encounter each day.

5

SPINE SERVICE

ANGELA FREEHILL BROWN, MD

I was running late, per my usual routine. I had hit snooze one too many times on this dreary February Saturday, and when I realized it, I was already behind. I threw on my scrubs, splashed water on my face and pulled my hair back in a ponytail grimacing in the mirror. It would have to do. No one was going to be looking at my face anyway. I was just a faceless worker bee in the sea of residents at the massive hospital where I worked.

"Oh no,'" I moaned and spoke out loud to myself. "Why didn't you get up early to read?" All of a sudden, I was anxious, realizing we had neurosurgery conference after rounds. I had so much to do and there was not going to be an extra second to spend cramming for this joint orthopedic and neurosurgery conference I had not prepared for. I was on my 4th year spine rotation in my ortho residency, and so far it had been drudgery. The cases were so long and frankly, I hated just standing around watching all the time. I really didn't want to be dissecting out nerve roots and extruded disks, but that was better than just standing around or doing paperwork or scut work. It was only my second week of my six week service, and I was already counting down the days until my hand rotation, which I hated just a tiny bit less than spine. The only bright spot was that I had a cool fellow on my team that week, and he occasionally let me do some things in the OR. I was looking forward to doing the anterior approach to the cervical spine later this week. It gave me butterflies, even early in the morning, to think about actually making an incision and dissecting down into someone's neck. The neck was such a vulnerable part of a person. I wasn't sure I was going to be able to do it.

I sped down the interstate in my old Honda Civic, music off, musing to myself. It was still pitch black at 5:22 am with no hint of the winter sunrise to come. I swung into a guest parking lot grateful that no attendants monitored this lot on Saturdays. It was the closest lot to the hospital, and technically I wasn't supposed to park there. Something had to give this morning, and this was a rule I didn't mind breaking today.

I trotted into the hospital, shucking my sweatshirt mid-walk and shimmying into my white doctor's coat. I still sometimes felt like an impostor wearing this thing, but at least it signaled to some of the more observant in the world that I wasn't a nurse. Half of the time though, an older (typically male) patient would listen to me talk, pat my hand and say, "That's nice honey, now when can I speak with the doctor?"

I made it to the ortho floor and grabbed my list from the night before. I checked off the boxes as I looked at each patient's vitals and nodded to one of the night nurses walking by, and we both assessed the time. She was gratefully getting ready to go home after a night's work, and likely, when she came back tonight for her next shift, I would still be here. "Ugh," I thought to myself. "What I wouldn't give for a nice nap and a warm blanket." I yawned just thinking about it and had to will myself up to go check on the patients. There were only five this morning, and that was a huge bonus. Of course, since it was so early, I woke every single one of them up. I disliked this part, and I know they did too. But most were pleasant enough once they lost the disorientation of the resident morning rounds wake up.

"Mr. Williams, wake up! Mr. Williams!" I whispered as loudly as I could and gently rubbed his arm, watching his rhythmic breathing and checking out his collared neck and bandage peeking out from under. He flipped open his eyes, "What?" He looked alarmed. "Mr. Williams, good morning, I am so sorry to wake you. I am Dr. Freehill, the resident on the spine service. I helped your surgeon with your procedure yesterday, and I was just coming by this morning to check on you. How are you feeling? How is your pain today?" He was actually doing quite well, and after I checked his dressing, had him move his arms up and down, grip both of my hands, and stick his tongue out, I was done and moved on to the next patient. The entire encounter would take less than 3 minutes. The advantage to early morning rounds was that the patients were so sleepy that they usually didn't ask me any questions. Surgeons' rounds are perfunctory and efficient. Is the patient alive? Are they having pain? Are they eating, peeing, pooping? Can they move their extremities? That is about it. Not too complicated on the back end of things.

I scurried to the charts and scribbled my notes. No events overnight on any of the patients and nothing of consequence to report. This was, again, a small blessing. It was never fun to bring news of complications.

I met up with the fellow and the junior residents. Most of them had a coffee in hand, and everyone looked just as rough as I did. By Saturday most all of us were exhausted. After conference, everyone who was not on call could go home, and the lot of us would spend Saturday afternoons curled up in bed or on the couch recovering from the brutality of the week. I was not so lucky this day. We had a semi-urgent add-on case to do, and the fellow had asked me to stay and help.

Conference was challenging. I was no expert in ortho spine, and I knew next to nothing about neurosurgery. I sunk down in my chair in the back of the room shivering a little from the chill of the room and from nerves. I was the only woman in the room which was not unusual for me. I had one female co-resident, but of course, we were never on service together. We both continually reminded each other that we were bad-asses since we were only the fifth and sixth women in the history of our orthopedic residency program. I needed her. I adored her. She was indeed a bad-ass, brilliant, and an amazing resident. Most days, I felt like I was just hanging on, and I would sleep instead of read. She, on the other hand, would do the work and read the papers and try to whisper the answers to me during conference: none of which I usually understood. My strength lay in my people skills and my hands. I surely could talk to anyone and put them at ease. I could do a mean arthroscopy; however, here in neurosurgery conference though, that wasn't going to help me.

"Dr Freehill," my reverie was broken, my heart plummeted, and I sat up straight in my chair. "Can you tell us please about the difference between the Hangman's fracture and a Jefferson fracture?" I stuttered an answer out, about the base of the C2 and the ring of C1, and thankfully, I had it nominally right and was given a pass. I prayed no further questions came my way, and I was lucky to survive the remainder.

After conference, it was time for a quick team breakfast. I hated coffee because it made me so jittery, but all of my team headed for the coffee cart at the entrance to the hospital. I relied on coffee as a rescue med of sorts. When I hadn't slept for nearly 24 hours, and I could feel my head get heavy and my eyelids pull inexorably down, coffee could give me a couple hours of improved alertness. This Saturday was still young so I decided to forgo the caffeine jolt, and I grabbed a bagel instead. We then chatted about the case.

This was a woman who presented to the office yesterday complaining of sudden onset of excruciating pain radiating into her hand and thumb. Her pain was severe such that she hadn't slept in two days, and she was kind of a wreck crying and carrying on in the clinic. I tried so hard not to judge the hysterical ones. I personally had never had anything more than a headache so all of the claims of such terrible pain were foreign to me. There were days though, when I surely thought that some of these people had just lost their damn minds, and that they weren't really having pain at all.

When I had first met her, I lumped this woman in as just one of the crazies, but the attending had sent her for a stat MRI. Looking at it later, sure enough she had a massive disk herniation at her C5-6 level. I was amazed, not at the disk herniation, but at my attending's ability to see beyond the histrionics to diagnose accurately a fixable problem. Mostly because of her nerve pain, but also because of the crying, the attending had put her on the schedule for today, Saturday, for an anterior cervical discectomy and fusion. This was quite unusual; I was coming to find out. The fellow coached me. "OK, Angela, today is your day. We are more relaxed today, and no cases to follow so I am going to guide you through the approach." I immediately perked up as anticipation jangled inside me.

It was rare as a resident that we actually got to pick up a knife and do real surgery. By fourth year, we were pretty expert at wound closure, but an approach to the cervical spine would be major for me. This was a surprise I hadn't planned, and of course, I hadn't read my anatomy yet. That was supposed to have been my Sunday project in between naps. My anxiety and excitement both rose exponentially. This was a fantastic chance though, and I couldn't blow it. "OK," I breathed. " Ok then, let's do it."

We made our way to the OR. The fellow went to change and get ready, and I grabbed the med student and went to the pre-op staging area. On a weekday this place would be buzzing, but today, it was just our patient and her nurse, and the lights were low. The typical blare of the beeping monitors was less, and I appreciated that our nurse had the insight to turn the volume down. I chatted with the med student about the importance of the history and physical on the patient's chart which I had carried a spare copy of in my coat pocket, just in case someone had lost the original. I had been burned before, and I never would have that happen again. I told him, "Now we always have to check the consent, the pre-op meds, and the patient's allergies then put our initials on the surgical site." I scanned the chart, and all looked good on my end.

I did a quick introduction with our patient, reminding her that we had seen her just the night before in the clinic. She was calm, entirely different from how she presented yesterday. I told her that her surgeon would see her right before she went back to surgery, but that we were just checking her papers and making sure all was in order. She smiled weakly, shaking her head "no" when I asked if she had questions. She closed her eyes, dismissing us, and we slipped away to get changed for surgery.

In the locker room, I changed quickly into clean, hospital-washed scrubs. I put my hair into a bun, and put my little blue bouffant hat on my head, carefully tucking in stray strands of hair then I put on my surgical shoe covers, just in case. I sat on the bench in front of the locker and took a deep breath. I didn't like spine, but I understood the significance of this step I was taking. I was about to take a scalpel and cut into this woman's neck. With precise dissection and the most care, we were going to enter her cervical spine and take away that disk material that was pinching on her nerve. We had the privilege of doing something so drastic as to enter her body and remove the cause of her pain. This was what I loved so much about surgery. I loved the swift and decisive fixing of things. I loved the satisfaction of repairing what was broken and seeing function return. So much of medicine in other fields was fascinating but with no real ability to impact a patient's life like this. I had loved neurology for the anatomy, but when it came time to treat the patient, there were so many syndromes where all we could do was say how sorry we were. Surgery fed a longing in me to fix the broken things and somehow make the world right.

I stepped to the scrub sink, mask on, glasses adjusted just right, turned on the water with my knee, and started the ritual washing. I remembered the first time I had done this as a medical student and how I had carefully counted out the washing strokes of each finger. Now, it was just a habit like brushing my teeth or tying a shoe. I just knew how to do it without thinking.

The scrub nurse gowned and gloved me, and carefully the fellow and I draped the patient. I was fascinated how a person looking so vulnerable transformed into a sterile surgical field just by the application of these blue drapes. It was necessary, at least for me, for the human-ness to fade so I could concentrate on the surgical task at hand.

The fellow guided me as I gripped the cold blade of the scalpel. I made my incision, and the bright droplets of blood sprang to the surface of the skin edges. Carefully, I spread the skin and subcutaneous tissue apart, revealing the pink muscle planes below. Palpating the muscle bellies and bluntly dissecting with my fingers, I was able to pull them apart. The fellow inserted a retractor, and within a minute or two there it was. The thin layer of fascia overlying the C5 vertebral body gleamed at me, and I felt a thrill of accomplishment rush through me. I had done it. I could feel my eyes twinkling with delight as I smiled under my mask. I handed my instruments back to the nurse and just then, the attending walked in. He glanced at me and stepped to the table. I was dismissed without a word more. It didn't matter though. Today, I was a surgeon. Today, I had made a difference. I had taken a real step toward my future, and I hadn't faltered. As I left the OR, hearing the real work of the surgery beginning, my steps were light and my vision clear. I could see my future. I knew that I was on my way to just where I belonged.

❧ 6 ❧

THE NECKLACE

JULIA DRY KNARREBORG, MD

I t was a bright yellow foam rubber cross on a thin white string. There were symmetric rainbow colored beads on each side. My son beamed from ear to ear while presenting me the unfinished necklace. I smiled and breathed a heavy sigh of relief. After three years of single parenting while in medical school and several recent call nights away from home, this small but precious gift meant my little guy still loved me and gave me permission to continue on our journey. Though I was never convinced we would actually finish it.

In my mind, the list of personal failures grew daily, permanently etched into my visual cortex so I constantly reviewed it. I tirelessly hedged every second of the day, afraid to make or miss the one move which would ultimately expose what I perceived to be my fraudulent existence. I teared up while clumsily tying the ends of this cheaply-made string into a crude knot then forming a necklace. I tried to precisely cut off the long string tips behind the knot, but the remaining ends frayed instantly, engraving yet another tick mark into the failures list enslaving my brain. I delicately placed the finished necklace around my neck, and I cupped my son's face in my hands and smiled, hoping he was still too young to interpret this particular pained fallback smile, one which had served me well during both parenthood and medical school. I hoped the exaggerated upturned corners of my mouth over-compensated for the worry and fear in my eyes. I worried the fraying I caused or the knot I tied would make this beautiful gift meet an untimely demise. I feared my work and mother-hood hazards would convert the foam rubber cross into an irregular fragment similar to a shred of tire tread. I somehow mustered the insight to allow myself to wear the necklace daily without regard and would address its eventual departure similar to how I addressed the passing of the first sluggish bagged goldfish my son won at a school carnival or the disappearance of his beloved blankie.

Many weeks and several months passed, and the necklace surprisingly remained intact. Several gray smudges now tainted the bright yellow color of the cross caused by me since I never stopped to wash my hands before clutching it. The back of the white string turned yellow brown similar to the inside collar of my white coat. Again from me because I never stopped to wash my neck after a code or rounds in the un-airconditioned hospitals. I carefully removed the necklace after each shift and — with only one exception — before each shift carefully slipped it over my head again, gently pulling my unruly hair through it before forming a tangled bundle I referred to as a bun.

Friends, patients, and strangers asked me daily about the necklace, and they smiled as I proudly described its sweet creator while clasping the cross between my thumb and fore-finger. Inevitably, during the story my eyes either watered with incomplete, hesitant tears of hope as I dreamed of easier days to come for our little family, or I stared blankly for a second or two as the chaotic thoughts of parenting and medical training ricocheted off the walls of my brain like pinballs. The end of the story usually snapped me out of each trance, and I instinctively touched the necklace and carried on with my day.

As the months passed and the necklace had not, I grew more attached to my prized gift and less willing to wear it without regard. I was afraid to pull the string too hard or even wash it. I was afraid to forget it each day, as not only was it proof my son still loved me but wearing it had somehow become the only way of proving to my son that I loved him. My fear eventually turned to reality the day I realized the necklace wasn't on me. I was sure it was in the washing machine, unraveling and disintegrating in the murky water product of bleach and black dust coating the city we lived in. My heart physically hurt as I pictured the string and its decorations lying in fragments at the bottom of the drum. Frantic devastation caused me to lose focus on my medical school professor and focus instead on how much I had failed my son and hated myself. What would I tell him that night when he enthusiastically asked me about the necklace's daily adventures during his bedtime story?

When I returned home, I raced upstairs to find it completely intact in my dirty, dry scrub pocket. Not only had I forgotten to check my pockets – I had forgotten to turn on the machine. "Sleep deprivation did have some benefits," I muttered to myself. I considered briefly trying to sand away a tick mark, but no — forgetting to turn on the machine was also technically a failure.

Many more months and soon two years passed, and the necklace remained intact. Dark black smudges coated nearly the entire outward-facing side of the cross. The cross edges were rounded instead of angled. The entire once white string was now a splotchy cappucino brown. Dirt and imperfections mottled the beads. Maybe I wasn't washing my hands or showering as often as I thought. That morning, however, after I showered, I even applied lip gloss and light brown concealer to hide the circles under my eyes. I had just finished a grueling month in the ICU and felt like rejoining in the land of the relatively fresh and clean. My unruly hair dried naturally, leaving the long curls to shed and stick to the back of my white coat; hairs that were plucked away by the lucky few residents sitting behind me during our morning conferences.

As I delicately put on the necklace and walked into the hospital, I remembered my favorite ICU patient. I had helped resuscitate this young father for 90 minutes prior to his ICU admission. He miraculously survived but hadn't regained consciousness so I came to know him through his family over the following weeks. Stories from his wife and sons mirrored those of life with my dad and stepfather, pillars of fortitude in their own rite. I couldn't imagine seeing either of them so weak and vulnerable, much like the knot and frayed string ends holding my necklace together. My patient's family asked about the necklace, and I showed them the dirty smudges, chipped beads and imperfect ends while telling "the story." In spite of its appearance, they loved the necklace and my son for making it. I voiced my surprise at its long survival. They voiced their hope for their dad to just survive.

I remember feeling shallow and frivolous at that moment, having allowed myself to place such importance on an accessory. But, to me at that time, it had become tangible proof that I was actually alive; I never allowed myself to really feel anything. Feelings might lead to weakness, weakness to more imperfection, and more imperfection to abject failure without return, recourse, or recompense. It was tangible proof that my son still loved me in spite of my maniacal yet exhausting, extreme yet monotonous existence as the perfect failure of a mom and medical student. This love kept me moving forward at times I wanted to give up, and, like stars in the sky, there were too many times to count.

I remembered randomly hearing of an incident in psychiatry in which a long necklace was used to choke a student. After hearing that, a recurring nightmare haunted my already disturbed sleep – the weak, frayed necklace string around my neck snapped under tension and its adornments flew through the air, landing in places visible by sight but impossible to reach. I woke up desperate for air each time. I realized over time that becoming a physician felt this way to me as I literally and figuratively held my breath, waiting for the other shoe to drop when "the real me" was exposed because I either failed to finish training or absolutely failed as a mom, officially ruining my son and our relationship because of my career choice. Simply touching the necklace prompted me to breathe, or teleported my son to my side or into my arms during a busy weekend call, reminding me why I chose this grueling path and him allowing me to see the sick people who needed mommy more than he did. At least that's what I convinced myself. Showered and alert, that morning otherwise started like many others - fondly remembering a patient or moment with my son but quickly morphing into one of many suffocating episodes of self-deprecation. I surfaced, gasping for air, when the page operator snapped me out my daze in the locker room just five minutes after I arrived. "Code blue, ICU, Code blue, ICU, Code blue, ICU."

I raced down the stairs because as fate would have it, my first day back on the wards was a call day and required immediate response to all codes. I slammed the button to open the automatic doors and rounded the corner to CPR in progress on my favorite patient. The breath was sucked out my lungs like an entire galaxy through a black hole. I jolted to a stop as if hitting a brick wall and bent over at the waist, hands on my knees to catch my breath. Then my hands grasped the necklace as I walked into his room. I started chest compressions pushing hard and fast with long strands of hair falling into my face with each cycle, distracting me as they flew up my nose and tickled my face. The rubber cross bounced off my chest and against my cheeks and lips, sticking momentarily to my thick clear lip gloss. Sweat beads formed, and the tears quickly followed. They flooded down my cheeks like a waterfall, and I hoped just one would land on my patient's chest, penetrate his skin to reach his soul, and revive him like the princess in the animated movie I had watched with my son the night before. Instead, they absorbed into gloss-glued strands of hair sponge and accumulated on my glass lenses.

Muscles achy and tired, my colleague replaced me and began pushing even harder on my patient's chest. I then moved to the back of the line of doctors, all waiting for their turn to give compressions. I took off my glasses and frantically but unsuccessfully fumbled in my white coat pockets for a hair tie. Without thinking, I ripped off my necklace and used it like a rubber band to secure my hair. The string stretched and knot tightened as I twisted it and wound it round and round, causing images from my nightmare to flash in my brain. I put my glasses on the window sill causing my tears to fall freely. I had now nothing in my way to prevent me from giving "perfect" CPR compressions.

I looked around the small room at the blurry medical staff who all looked like angels with specific jobs, all designed to work in harmonious steps to save a life. I wished I could do more. I prayed continuously and reached for my necklace several times, only to remember it was now somehow strongly holding my hair together while stretched to its limits in what I had thought was its most weak and vulnerable state. I watched the skin of this once vibrant young father lose color and limbs of this once strong husband remain lifeless, only mobile through our efforts to revitalize them. I looked down at the embroidered name on my white coat and wondered why I deserved the initials at the end. Nearby, brown-tinged wet strokes remained on my coat where concealer-mixed tear-soaked hair tips brushed. I arrived again at the front of the compression line, naively determined to save this precious being with falling tears and better CPR now that my hair was pulled back and my glasses removed.

I don't remember the exact time of death. All I remember hearing is, "time of death, 7..." followed by muffled whispers similar to ones I had heard at a funeral one year prior. I hadn't cried in years, and at that moment sheer will and my large, clumsy hands mentally and physically forced back sobs and screams as my legs somehow found their way to the break room. In the doorway, a medical student I barely knew reached with arms wide open, and I fell into them weeping uncontrollably, subconsciously pulling my arms in against my chest to touch the necklace, causing her to support my full weight and sorrow. A few minutes passed, and my legs slowly stood up and walked me to the nurses' station.

"Please let me know when his wife and sons arrive," I muttered to his nurse with my head hanging low in shame and sadness. She cupped my face in her hands, lifted it up, and I immediately recognized the pained smile which I'm sure – like me – had served her well over the years. I don't remember walking out of the ICU and up the stairs to meet my new patients. My necklace somehow made it out of my hair and around my neck. Soft fleeting whimpers emerged intermittently and uncontrollably from my body in the stair-well, hallways, and nurses' stations. About thirty minutes passed when I got the call, I walked down to the ICU terri-fied to face his family because I had committed the ultimate failure – I couldn't save him.

I took off my white coat before pulling back the curtain. I wanted them to see the necklace and to see me as family rather than a physician. We sat quietly together across from the bed and cried. They told me they didn't blame me as they reached for my dirty yellow cross, the only color remaining in the sepia-colored, dimly lit room. "Go home and hug your son. He loves you more than you know."

When I left the ICU for the second time that morning, I could breathe, and for the first time since the moment I first saw my son, I felt alive. I realized how great a feat my once-sheltered necklace had performed in securing my thick, crazy hair during what must have felt like a wooden roller coaster ride. It wasn't designed to tie back tresses, and it didn't perfectly hold them like something designed for that specific purpose would have. But by protecting the necklace, I never fully tested it. By never fully testing it, I never witnessed its true strength. By never witnessing its true strength, I never realized its full potential. Without realizing its full potential, it likely could not fail, but it positively could not live and neither could I. My entire life up to that point I had avoided failure like the plague, but after leaving my patient's room that day I not only redefined failure, I welcomed it. I realized that without failure there would never be an opportunity for grace. And without grace, there could and would never be "good enough."

That day I freed myself. I freed myself from this bright yellow foam rubber cross on a thin, white string, once a representation of my hidden, exhaustingly average existence also called perfectionism and precariously teetering, fickle self worth and insecurity as a harried mom and physician in training. My necklace was good enough. I was good enough. Imperfection wasn't failure and didn't define purpose or success or qualify worth.

MANY, MANY YEARS HAVE NOW PASSED, AND THE NECKLACE

remains intact. The crude knot is tighter than ever – too tight to undo with even the smallest, sharpest edge. Stretching it actually secured it. The once thin white string is now rusty brown and thinner but somehow stronger, and the ends are no longer frayed. Over time, impurities from my unwashed hands, fingers, and hair had smoothed the material, acting like glue. The entire side of the cross facing outward is black, but it now sparkles with glitter after bouncing off of my lip gloss during that fateful code blue.

My son and I still talk about the necklace and its adventures every now and then. As I was dropping him off at school one morning while writing this story, I asked him if he remembers being lonely while I was working, or if he felt he had a bad childhood because of what I chose to pursue. He said, "No, mom. All I remember is how happy I was when I saw you again." He paused, and then looked back at me smiling while heaving his heavy backpack over his shoulders.

Today, my necklace lies not around my neck in a nervous and obsessive attempt to protect it. It lies in a drawer alongside used makeup and cotton balls. It no longer represents my daily attempts to avoid failure or reassure my worthiness. It represents life - the compilation of thousands of hours of truth and humanity and all of the good, bad, and ugly that comes along with them.

THE FAMILY BUSINESS

ARCHANA R. SHRESTHA, MD

As a teenager, Saturdays were often spent working in my mom's office. She was a solo physician who ran her own private family medicine practice. Over the years her family practice had become our family business. I would help out by filing away charts, answering phones, and scheduling appointments. My brothers would vacuum, collect trash and clean exam rooms. My dad was her practice manager and would do her billing. We all heard about the inner workings of what it was like to be a doctor including some of the calls Mom would get in the middle of the night from her patients. My mom would often take me with her to round on her patients in the hospital. After seeing them, we would stop by the cafeteria before going home, and she would buy me a treat, or if the cafeteria was closed, she would make me hot chocolate in the doctors' lounge.

When I worked in her office, her patients would be so excited to see me. They would say, "I remember when your mom was pregnant with you, and she had beautiful long hair past her waist. I'd come in for my annual physical, and for three years straight she was always pregnant. I couldn't believe it!"

My mom, born and raised in India, came to this country after she graduated from medical school. She wore her hair extremely long then, but as a young doctor, she cut it short, at the suggestion of my father, to come across as more professional. My mom would giggle and say, "We had three kids in three years, and at one point they were all in diapers. It was hard, but with the grace of God we made it through." She not only made it through, but she also managed to be a great doctor to her patients in the process.

"We love your mom," said one of her patients. "We have been coming to her forever. She saved my life, you know. Now, are you going to be a doctor like your mom so you can take over her practice one day when she retires?" they would often ask with a smile.

Yes, I would say. But, I never quite knew where or when the seed of becoming a doctor had been planted. It somehow had been a given that my brothers and I would all become doctors. I was doing well in school; I had always liked science and was a caring and kind individual. Medicine was the family business so it seemed the natural route to go. My parents had instilled in me how I must become a professional, be able to stand on my own two feet, and never have to depend on my husband or anyone else. Becoming a lawyer, business person, or engineer didn't interest me one bit.

So, by default, off I went to college as part of a program with a guaranteed admission to medical school. Everything was set. All I had to do was get my med school prerequisites done, graduate undergrad with good grades, and take the MCAT; then I would have a coveted medical school seat. But in undergrad, confusion set in. Was I becoming a doctor because I had chosen to, or was I becoming one because it was what I'd always been told to do?

During college I began to explore other areas that interested me. I played college tennis for a year, but then the demands of NCAA Division 1 sports became too much to maintain with my coursework so I decided not to play a second year. Since I had always loved writing, and journalism seemed exciting, in my newly found free time I joined the university's newspaper and began to write about sports.

I quickly fell in love with journalism and loved covering sports; I loved getting to go behind the scenes at college sporting events and interviewing people for my articles. And then, one day a professional tennis tournament came to our university, and I was lucky enough to cover it. I sat in the press box next to journalists from the Chicago Tribune, CNN and ESPN. I got to meet and ask questions of Venus and Serena Williams at a press conference. From that moment on, I was hooked!

"I might want to be a journalist and not a doctor after all," I thought. All I knew was I felt drawn to pursue journalism further. After I finished my undergraduate degree instead of starting medical school, I convinced my parents I was going to get a one-year master's degree in journalism and then would go to medical school. The medical college had agreed to hold my spot for me.

"Why do you want to waste your time with that?" my parents asked but somewhat reluctantly agreed and respected my decision. They knew how much I enjoyed writing and that I excelled at it.

I moved away from home for journalism school and into a graduate student dorm. Although it was about three hours away, it was the first time I'd ever lived so far away from home, and I didn't know a single person there. In my first journalism class at grad school my professor said, "If you want to become a good journalist, you must become comfortable with talking to people." While he said that to the whole class,

I felt he was talking directly to me. As a small child I'd been one to hide behind my mother's sari holding on to her leg at Indian social events, and in high school, I was known as a somewhat reserved kid and often described as quiet.

I took what my professor said to heart and started talking to everyone especially at my dorm's social nights. Within a few weeks, I had become the social butterfly of the entire dorm. Most everyone knew who I was, and I made lots of friends in a short period of time. I had completely come out of my shell, and I was in love with this new person I had found. I was also doing lots of interviews, writing great articles, getting my work published in magazines and even getting paid for some of my work. I started to wonder, should I even go to med school? I was having the time of my life in journalism school.

As the second semester was winding down, I began to write my master's thesis article. Conflicted about what I should do about my medical school admission, I decided to write about physician satisfaction in medicine. I set out to interview a variety of doctors in all sorts of specialties and at different points in their careers. I looked at the research and the surveys done of doctors, and the answer was looking grim. Doctors didn't seem to be all that satisfied with the medical profession once they were out in practice: there were the HMO's, PPO's and Medicare rules; billing hassles along with sometimes upset patients; as well as the doctor's lifestyle and the huge medical school debt. Doctors were feeling bogged down and barely able to do what they had set out to do -- to simply heal and care for patients.

But in the swarm of all that data, I would close my eyes, and certain images would come to mind: images of being in my mother's office and seeing how much she meant to all her patients. What stood out to me were those days working in my mother's office and all the times her patients would say how much they loved her, how she had helped them so much, and how she was like a family member to them. I recalled how she received presents from them on her birthday and how she would get invited to their weddings, to their birthdays, and to the funerals when the inevitable happened. She had truly made an impact on her patients' lives.

What I discovered was that physicians were dissatisfied with the business side of running a practice, but many of them truly did still love the practice of medicine and the care of patients. They loved the moments where it was just them and a patient in a conversation one-on-one, and they had a chance to serve them, to help them and to heal them. That was the practice of medicine.

One of my journalism professors knew about my predicament and the seat awaiting me in medical school. "You must choose. You are a talented journalist and writer, but if you go into medicine, you will be too busy, and you will never find your way back to writing," he warned.

I decided that I needed to know for myself what it was like to be a physician, not for my parents nor anyone else. I wanted to become a doctor. I felt called to become a healer and help others through medicine. I knew that if I didn't do it, I would regret not having become a doctor and wonder what would have been if I had gone to medical school.

The writing would always be there, I thought. I can write while in medical school or after. There are plenty of doctors who write books or articles, and I can too. I knew I would find my way back to it one way or another, and that the experiences I would have practicing medicine could give me so much to write about. So, I made up my mind that I wanted to take care of people and have hands that could heal them. I wanted to make my life's work about helping others through health and wellness.

I submitted my master's thesis and walked across the

stage to collect my journalism degree knowing that even though I was now off to medical school, every second of what I had learned in journalism school was worth it. I had grown, matured and had discovered a whole new side of myself. Little did I know at the time that medicine and journalism had some similarities. I would see in medical school that they also called it "interviewing" when you talk to a patient; that you must be adept at speaking to people of all different walks of life; and that in medicine too, you must be bold and confident and ask the hard and sometimes uncomfortable questions of patients.

While high school, undergrad, and even grad school had been relatively easy sailing for me, and I was always in the top of my class, in medical school, I had truly met my match. I stumbled, felt challenged and as though I was trying to drink from a fire hydrant. There was just too much information coming at us at once, and it was the most difficult thing I had ever done. In the first two years of medical school we learned anatomy, physiology, pharmacology, pathology, genetics and more. We dissected cadavers, brains and did simulation labs on live animals. In the process, we learned the equivalent of an entire new language. While medical school was extremely hard, now that I had committed to this path, I persisted and studied harder than I ever had in my life. I made lots of sacrifices so that I could pass my classes and board exams.

After two years, we were let out of the classroom and laboratories and out onto the hospital wards. It was then that I started to fall in love with medicine. I enjoyed nearly every rotation I did from obstetrics to pediatrics, to surgery and family medicine. I kept changing my mind as to which specialty I should choose for residency. Then I decided I should do an emergency medicine rotation because in the ER, I knew they dealt with everything from pediatrics to geriatrics, and urgent care to critical care. They also got to do procedures which I had enjoyed doing on my surgical rotation. Whenever I went to the ER, the emergency physicians seemed like everyday heroes truly saving people's lives.

It turned out emergency medicine was a great fit for me. The same excitement that had drawn me to journalism also drew me to the emergency department. I liked being on the front line taking in all the action. I also loved that emergency doctors just focused on the care of the patient. It didn't matter if patients could pay or if they had insurance. They were all treated the same. I liked that I didn't have to deal with the business side of medicine, and I could just purely take care of people in their true moment of need.

I made up my mind that I would do emergency medicine and told my clerkship director that I wanted to apply for emergency medicine residency. When I told him, he asked me about my board scores, looked me in the eye, and told me I would never match into a spot and that I didn't have what it took to be an emergency physician. I knew I didn't have the highest board scores, but I wasn't going to let him crush my hopes of getting into the one field that felt so right for me.

So, I did what I do best. I buckled down and worked harder and smarter. I found other ways to stand out. I did an elective rotation in toxicology, made sure I stood out as a star student, and as a result received a glowing recommendation from the emergency medicine residency program director. I was invited to emergency medicine residency interviews, and the people skills I learned in journalism school helped me to interview well. I made sure to highlight all my other extracurriculars as president of my college's chapter of American Medical Student Association, my research as a Fulbright fellow, and my health policy work. Other people might have higher test scores than me, but I knew I was well-rounded and had unique experiences that no one else had. More importantly, I knew I would be a fantastic emergency physician not just because I had the brains for it, but also because I had the people skills for it.

Then, it was Match Day. I stood in the beautiful hall my school had arranged for Match Day, and when my name was called I was nervous to open up my envelope to find out if I had obtained a spot in emergency medicine residency, and if so, where. I held my breath as I opened my envelope.

As I read the letter, a huge smile grew on my face. I had done it! I had matched in emergency medicine and to my number one choice of emergency medicine residency programs. I never did get to speak with the emergency medicine clerkship director who told me I wouldn't match, but I really wanted to tell him that he had been wrong. I could get into emergency medicine residency and into an excellent program too.

છત્ર

It's been fourteen years since I graduated medical school, but that act of proving that clerkship director wrong has been a source of so much strength in my life. And, as I sit here writing, I think back to my journalism professor who told me I likely would never come back to writing, but here I am writing a chapter for this book.

Coming from a family of doctors, sometimes people ask me if I tell my kids to become doctors. What I tell my children is this – "Be anything you'd like to be. You don't have to follow in your parents' footsteps. You are free to follow your intuition and see where it leads you, but be sure to listen to your heart because it could be your future self calling you to where you are meant to go."

Deciding to be a doctor was the right choice for me. I love my career in emergency medicine and have also found a way to incorporate writing in my life. Sometimes the path we take is not one others have traveled before or one that others can understand. Mine has been windy, but it was my own path. It was a path I needed to take to ensure I was making the right decisions in my life. My choices have taken me to many great places and taught me so much. Just because others couldn't see a straight line to a destination, doesn't mean that a windy path couldn't be paved.

❧ 8 ❧

TITLES

MARIA PEREZ-JOHNSON, DO, FAAP

Just a small town girl, livin' in a lonely world...
She took the midnight train goin' anywhere...

Most of you, I hope, will recognize the above lyrics. They are part of a song from my era, my generation, which is listed as the greatest song of the 1980's. It's Journey's "Don't Stop Believing," and at least those first few words describe me.

I am a small town girl from South Texas. Bishop, Texas, is where I called home for many years and where I graduated as a Badger way back in 1985. It's funny though that at the ripe old age of 17, I thought I'd never return. Yet today and over the last few years I've been in the process of remodeling my eventual dream retirement home; a 1910 farmhouse, that sits just inside the very town to which I swore I'd never return; a house that I can't wait to move into.

So who am I, and why did I want to share my story in this forum? Well, I'm a lot of titles, and indeed titles make a daily difference even in the work I do. First of all, I'm female, I'm Hispanic, a Mexican American. I'm a mother, a parent, a spouse, a sister and a daughter. I'm a teacher, a physician, a doctor, a healer, a pediatrician, an emergency room doctor, and a DO (Doctor of Osteopathic Medicine). Each of these is me, and my hope is that maybe by sharing my journey it can one day inspire someone else to reach for the same. Maybe it could allow one small town girl to also achieve some of these titles as well.

So what is in a title, and what's in all the titles I behold? Let's take the first one.

I'm female.

It is and probably always will be a male dominated world, especially in medicine. On a daily basis at work, I get called: nurse, tech, Miss, Mrs.— anything except doctor. Yes, this horrific stereotyping is annoying on many facets. Not only do I have to wear the shield of my profession, but I also have to define it and prove that I am what my title states that I am.

Gender inequality and bias have received a lot of media attention recently; it exists everywhere and is profound even in the medical profession. As a female physician, not only am I often deprived of a title I've earned and worked hard for, but by being female I am also held to a different set of standards. I must dress nicely, maybe even in heels, and despite my shifts being twelve hours in length, my hair must be kept nicely. I must wear make-up as I've been told that customers, rather patients, prefer female doctors who wear appropriate make-up, not too much though; there is a balance. I'm not alone in this fight of gender equality. I'm not alone in this unfairness. Women across the nation, not only physicians, are aware of this. Change is hard, and it takes time.

I am also beyond privileged to have been given the opportunity to *shine on* as a female physician. I've served in leadership roles on medical staffs of hospitals and many departments. My medical school class was the first class with a 50/50 percent male to female enrollment, and now more and more female medical administrators are being tasked to lead both medical schools and medical boards across the nation. Unfortunately, even with these advances some still don't see women in this new progressive light.

A few weeks ago, a male nurse practitioner student was in the ER doing his clinical rotations. After presenting his patient, we went to the bedside where I performed my exam and assessment. Following my standard introduction and discussion of my findings with the family, they consistently addressed the student as doctor and myself as either ma'am or nurse. Despite my repeating that I indeed was the physician, they repeatedly failed to address me accordingly. This is due to the fact that in medicine:

• 70% of physicians are male.[1]

• Female physicians make half of a male physician's salary, but change is coming.[2]

• The proportion of women entering medicine has more than doubled since 1980.[3]

• More women practice pediatrics and gynecology than men — this is especially true for new doctors.[4]

• There are still a handful of specialties without many female doctors, including orthopedic surgery or urology.[4]

• Studies have proven that patients seen by a female physician fare better overall and have better health and better outcomes.[5]

I am Hispanic, a Mexican American.

I am proud of my heritage. I am a first generation college student and the first physician in my family. Now many of my cousins have also gone on to graduate from my own alma mater as well as other universities. We have teachers, lawyers, other doctors, nurses, and even a NASA engineer within our family tree now. Does ethnicity make a difference? Most definitely.

People want to be treated and cared for by those that can acknowledge their own beliefs and understand their own language. I've had the privilege of practicing in many areas. I served in the United States Air Force and practiced medicine in the United Kingdom. I've worked in many communities in Texas, along the Rio Grande Border, as well as in Nevada, Georgia, and Ohio. Each area has its unique climate and culture, and each is in dire need of great scientists and medical professionals. Medical professionals who can reach out to these communities and inspire them towards better health.

Here are the facts:

• Hispanic physicians make up close to 5% of all practicing physicians.[6]

• Only 5.5% of medical school graduates are Hispanic.[7]

I am family.

I am a mother, a parent, a spouse, a sister, and a daughter. Family is important; especially for times when this journey in life is difficult. Without the support of your kids, parents, or spouse it can be overwhelming to accomplish this task. You need your family, now and in the future. If you think you can do this alone, you're dead wrong. I wouldn't be here today if it were not for the countless sacrifices my parents, kids, and spouse have made and continue to make that allow me to do a job that I love — to practice in a profession that I'm passionate about.

A few years ago, after my kids were both away in college and medical school, I was feeling a bit of empty nest syndrome. I thought it would be a brilliant idea to take in a foreign exchange student. *Easy right? I'm technically gone half of the month, and when I am home I prefer to travel or sleep.* So when we were approved for a student from Brazil, I was ecstatic! Six months later, needless to say, it didn't quite work out.

He questioned why I would want a student around when I was never around. He challenged why we could be so unattached to his activities and events at school. He even said I cursed too much. "Like a sailor," he said. I corrected him and said "like a F$%*#ing Air Force major, thank you very much."

I honestly didn't realize I cursed that much...until he brought it up at the exit interview. When he left at midpoint in the semester, I was heartbroken for a bit, but not so much because he didn't fit into our...rather $M\Upsilon$ world, but because he had put into perspective what perhaps my own children had lived through. *WOW, is this what I gave up? Is this the torture that my own kids endured? In addition, is this the best marriage that I can have, the best relationship with my parents? Did I give up all that for this? A title, a job, a career.*

I don't have a 9-5 job. Nobody in medicine does. I have twelve hours locked away in a dungeon of an emergency room without a chance of ever leaving until my relief arrives. There is no calling in sick; there is no ability to leave early for my son's game or my daughter's birthday party. Whatever rolls through that door must be taken care of until an outcome is obtained even if it rolls in 10 minutes prior to end of my shift on the night of my anniversary dinner. My arrangements and work shifts are meticulously planned weeks to months in advance in order to ensure that everyone gets a piece of me. I also must remember to attempt to schedule some of my own free time to ensure that I can maintain my own sanity. Who suffers the most due to this crazy, hectic, and chaotic life of a physician? Most often it is those that we care about the most. OUR

FAMILIES. My days can be hard, harder than most people can ever imagine.

I'm a teacher, a physician, a doctor, a healer, a pediatrician, an emergency room doctor, a DO.

I guess I've always wanted to be a doctor. My parents will tell you that I wanted to be a doctor since I was two years old. Perhaps that is true; perhaps they had a little input. Most days, I love what I do, but some days are hard, as I stated above. The ability to see people at their best is phenomenal regardless of where you work; your work family will keep you sane. If this is the career that one aspires to do, similar to me, you will spend most of your time with your work family; weekends, holidays, and most evenings are shared with them. Twelve hours at work, a one hour commute, about six hours of sleep, and an hour to get ready leaves essentially two to four hours on the couch or some other activity to spend with those I love then I'm off to bed to repeat the cycle...and that's just when I work in town. If I'm traveling, I may not see my family for a week to twelve days at a time.

I am a teacher.

Physician AND doctor all mean teacher. Daily I teach medical students, pediatric residents, family practice residents, and emergency medicine residents. I teach my co-workers, PAs and NPs, and my scribes who are still in college. I also am obligated to teach the families of those I care for. I educate them on their illness, their outcomes, and their expected course of illness.

As a pediatrician, I have chosen to specialize in kids, that is kid's health. Kids indeed are wonderful and resilient. However, daily I have to fight the media and social misinformation to provide quality, evidence based medicine; I am, after all, a scientist first. Vaccines, viral illness, standards of care that prove or disprove care, all for the sake of what is in the patient's best interest can all be Googled online, fighting misinformation can often time be difficult. This is all while dealing...*or attempting to deal*...with the demands of a growing consumer mentality of medicine.

Can I provide quality care without caving in to the demands of my patient and parent population? Why must we continue to disprove false information about vaccines, antibiotics, nutrition, and even excessive studies, lab work or radiation exposures?

I'm a veteran.

I'm a veteran, a US Air Force Major, and a dependent of a US Navy sailor. Serving my country was one of the most fulfilling and painful endeavors I have experienced. Granted, it wasn't always the most fun, but I was able to explore so much more of this great planet. I was stationed and worked alongside individuals from all across this great nation. I moved from Del Rio, Texas, to the United Kingdom, where I lived and practiced for three years wearing the uniform; it was amazing. The respect and fortitude of those who serve should never be undervalued.

My children have a whole new perspective of the freedoms those who serve grant us by being raised in a military family, living in military housing, and having friends with people across the globe. The shared heartaches of deployments and time away from family are experiences only a military brat can understand: Reveille in the mornings, TAPS at night, and standing still during both of these events, even if you're on the playground, is something they will never forget. Bowling alley parties on base, the pool and rec halls, a movie theatre where the national anthem is played before each movie and everyone stands at attention, along with the unfathomable agony of learning that a loved one will not return from their deployment — these are all memories that a child of a military dependent could encounter.

Here are some additional statistics:

- Only 17% of officers in the armed forces are female.[8]
- When I left the US Air Force, I was 1 of 2400 female officers nationwide. Of that only 2% of those officers were Hispanic, thus I was 1 of only 48.

I am a non-traditional student.

I am a graduate of Texas A&M University Kingsville (TAMUK), a small university in South Texas that many will not know of, thus I am a Hog, a Javelina (my college mascots), and a Ron McNair Scholar. I am a non-traditional student. I graduated at 17, went to college, got engaged, was married, left college, traveled, and five years later started a family. Then three years following that, I decided to return to school to complete the education I started and to go off and attempt to become the physician that I always wanted to be.

I was hooded for my doctorate and will always think fondly of my mentor, my favorite professor Dr. John C. Perez, for which whom the Ron McNair Program, and the Natural Toxins Research Center would not be here. When I first returned to college, to TAMUK back in 1994, I met with Dr. Perez, whose words would resonate with me. The same words I would end up proving wrong.

After he asked me what I was there for and what my ultimate goal was, he told me on that mid-June day that my chances of getting into medical school were slim. In fact, he didn't think I would have a chance. I suspect he believed that I had been out of school for too long, and that I was now too old. I was married, I had kids, I was female, I was a minority, and I needed to improve my GPA. And, I was now needing to take advanced classes after a long break in my beginning courses. For a second I believed him, and for a moment after I failed my first immunology test that semester, I had doubt.

I went home, cried to my mom, cried in front of the kids, and questioned why I would leave my husband in another state and move halfway across the country to pursue this foolishness. I gave up a nice home, a career in banking that I had established, loaded up a U-Haul, and moved back to achieve what now seemed impossible. I went to work and ended up with an A in immunology as well as in every other course I took until I graduated in December of 1997. I graduated magna cum laude with a BS degree in biology and a minor in chemistry. I was accepted to Texas College of Osteopathic Medicine in Fort Worth. So yes, I'm a DO (doctor of osteopathic medicine). I'm board certified in pediatrics and have practiced pediatric emergency medicine at various children's hospitals in Texas, Ohio, Nevada, and Georgia.

杘

SO THIS SHORT STORY HAS BEEN ALL ABOUT ME – BUT IT CAN be about any one who is reading this. Many of the titles I've held can also define anyone. Titles can also stifle you, suppress you, hold you back, encase and enslave you if you let them. Each of these titles could have incapacitated me and not allowed me to become successful. Each, in its own way, could have prevented me from pursuing my dream. Yet, each title is a badge, a shield. Every single one of them defines me and makes me a better practitioner. They shape how I see the world, and often times how the world sees and treats me.

What should you take out of this chapter?

Nothing and Everything.

- It is really all about you. Take and learn from others. In medicine we have a saying, "To gain experience: YOU MUST SEE ONE, DO ONE, AND THEN TEACH ONE."
- I'm a simple girl from a small town.
- Don't let anyone tell you that you can't – if you believe them, YOU won't.
- Anything and everything is possible.
- Pause and wait. IT CAN BE DONE.
- You define your outcome – choose happiness.
- Prejudice will always be there – how you handle it defines you.
- What you do now matters – life happens. It has a roundabout way to get you to your destination; life is not always a straight line.
- Remember where you came from – the best memories and moments come from there.

❧ 9 ❧

ROSE DAY

SURABHI BATRA, MD, AND VINOD K. BATRA, MD

It was a misty morning of February in India, and I got up early as usual to arrive at my clinic on time. Incidentally, it was the 14th of February - Valentines Day - a day people exchange flowers and good wishes with their loved ones. I hurried up with morning chores, had a quick breakfast, and drove my car to the hospital. Today was our procedure day, and the nurses in charge had scheduled almost a dozen endoscopies for the same routine problems: hemorrhoids, polyps, malignancies, and inflammatory bowel disorder (IBD). As I came out after a procedure and changed my gown, I saw a young girl waiting for me with a rose in her hand. "Doctor, how did it go for my mother Rosemary?" I encouraged her to wait until the histopathology report was finalized and walked to my chamber. I was suddenly pushed into my thoughts, five years before...Her name was Rose.

I WAS THE CHIEF RESIDENT, AND IT WAS OUR ADMISSION day. We had our clinics in the morning and were busy as usual once stepping back on the hospital floors. The admissions from the ER poured in with multiple problems that were cared for by my teammates to the best of their ability. After all the admissions were assessed by me personally, we began getting ready for the rounds with the unit head, Dr. Mathew.

As I came out of the ER after seeing another patient, I noticed a young girl who was not particularly sick looking, but something about her disturbed eyes caught my attention. I was compelled to halt in my steps more as a surprise than to offer any medical assistance. She was dressed as if going to attend a wedding and was perhaps accompanied by her parents. Her name was Rose; she was 19 years old.

The presenting complaint was bleeding from her rectum for at least the last day, weakness and dizziness. She appeared pale, and her eyes were swollen as if she had been crying. The residents' provisional diagnosis of colitis/hemorrhoids after a normal rectal examination and proctoscopy where a scope visualized inside her colon didn't require any confirmation now. She was given treatment to help with her symptoms and moved on to the wards. I had a glance at her, but her eyes and facial expression did arouse my curiosity. It appeared from her eyes as if she wanted to say something.

I finished my duty and signed off in the morning. Back home I could not get her off my mind. Her attractive face, a beautiful girl with no apparent disease...why should she have bleeding? What were her eyes saying to me? I had no answers. I waited until the next morning and was on the floor before time. After a brief routine round, I started rounding with Dr. Mathew's as usual discussing the patients we cared for. I was nowhere mentally present in the rounds and was perhaps waiting for this girl to be examined. We finished in one section of the ER and moved on to the one where she was. My eyes were looking for her and finally the team of doctors reached her bed. We asked the same routine questions: history, family history, as well as past and personal history then completed the examination. This was followed by a provisional diagnosis of colitis, hemorrhoids, and a polyp, and routine investigations were ordered. We all moved on despite my wish to try to figure out what was it that was bothering her. The afternoon was filled with routine work, and I could not get a chance to speak to her. I went home and started reviewing different causes of bleeding from the rectum. I was very concerned and disturbed. The causes ranged from simple colitis to cancer. I didn't know why I was getting more worried and concerned.

Five days passed, and there were no signs of improvement nor were there any leads to diagnosis. We sent her for a colonoscopy the next morning, and that put to rest everyone's guess work. She had extensive acute ulcerations of her entire colon sparing her sigmoid colon to some extent: this explained a normal proctosigmoidoscopy (a direct inspection of the rectum and the sigmoid colon using a sigmoidoscope). The biopsy was sent for a histopathology report to look at the tissue on a microscopic level, and the treatment protocol for her newly diagnosed ulcerative colitis was then started. A sense of gloom prevailed on Rose as well as her parents after learning about the diagnosis, its treatment, and various outcomes in the presence of no definite external cause. I don't know why I got more and more interested and attached to her. She rarely spoke and looked depressed and mostly lost in her thoughts.

One day while on a visit during visitors' hours, I saw her having a massive argument with her parents who were almost shouting, and she was crying! It was an unusual happening as relatives mostly are affectionate to their sick relatives. Not to disturb them, I thought of talking to Rose the next day.

The next few days kept me busy and finally on a Sunday morning visit, I found the opportunity to speak to Rose at length. On the way to the hospital, I bought some flowers which I gave to her while wishing her good morning. I was surprised and upset to learn that there was no improvement in her symptoms. I sat on the sofa beside her, sent my team off, and started the conversation.

"What was happening the other day between you and your parents?" I asked her.

She gave a surprised smile and said in a balanced tone, "They are worried about my marriage."

"Well, that's not unusual Rose." I said in a surprised tone.

"That cannot be the reason of such an argument?" I asked firmly. She broke down suddenly and narrated that which was not only surprising but painful.

Rose was the eldest of the three daughters to her parents. Her father had a small job which could hardly sustain the family. The parents were orthodox and didn't believe in higher education or employment for girls. Rose had a lonely childhood and was an introvert throughout as she had minimum communication with her parents, siblings, or school mates. She was a brilliant student with excellent scores in fine arts throughout her schooling and was currently in her final year of undergrad with aspirations to go abroad for further education. Her father was always opposing her and had arranged her marriage to a small business boy without her agreement or consent. They had repeated arguments and fights and in the last few months; she was even physically beaten. Her mother had no say and agreed to the father's wishes silently.

Rose was under constant stress and was to be married the day after her present admission into the hospital. Her symptoms of ulcerative colitis appeared for the first time on the night prior to her scheduled marriage. The marriage was now rescheduled for the following month. This was the argument between her and her parents.

Rose was shedding tears throughout her narration. It was

with difficulty that I had to stop the conversation and make her comfortable with the help of the nurse on duty. I left with the assurance that all shall be well and that she would stop worrying. I knew very well that stress can surely precipitate many a disease symptoms, and thus took it upon myself to speak to her parents.

I sent a request to her parents to meet the following Sunday; they agreed. Unfortunately, Rose's symptoms kept worsening despite adequate treatment. We engaged the services of a psychologist too, but it didn't help. Meanwhile, I made it a habit to speak to Rose each day after my rounds to crack a joke or two and carry a single rose to her daily without fail. I saw her getting more vocal and cheerful and could clearly see a shine in her eyes. She was becoming more expressive and talkative.

The next week arrived, and I had an extensive talk with her parents. They thought that it was a minor disease and would settle down after she was married and became more responsible. They were initially considering that she was malingering as a way to avoid marriage. I had to explain to them the gravity of the disease as well as its autoimmune nature causing the body to attack itself when triggered. I suggested that they cancel the marriage, let the girl choose her career, get healthier, and reconsider this matter at a later stage. Such a decision should help the disease regress.

They were initially not ready to budge but later agreed. I broke the news of them putting the marriage on hold to Rose. She was so happy and excited that she hugged me more than once and almost put a kiss on my cheeks. "You are a great doctor," were her words. I reached home victorious in a number of ways.

The next few days passed, and we saw an obvious improvement in her symptoms and reduced the dosage of her medicines. Her parents agreed to send her abroad for higher education and applied for student loans. They also agreed to allow her to marry the man of her choice.

As she was symptom free, I did a repeat colonoscopy, and to my utter surprise, there was no trace of the disease. She had recovered fully and was ordered to be discharged from the hospital. With discharge papers in her hand, I saw her holding a rose for me in her other hand. She had tears in her eyes, but this time they had a shine which was pleasingly grateful. I hugged her and took the rose to tuck it in my jacket.

Years later I heard that Rose is now well settled with the man of her choice in a far off place and is gainfully employed. She never had a recurrence of her symptoms.

...BACK TO THE WARDS, THE HISTOPATHOLOGY OF Rosemary was ready, and it showed "adenocarcinoma". Her little daughter still held a rose for me in her hand, but I had tears in my eyes. I gently lifted her to my chest and hugged her. I had no words on the ways of life and destiny. I looked at the sky and moved on to the next patient after ordering for Rosemary to be referred to surgery to treat and possibly remove the colon cancer.

10

WOMEN DON'T BELONG IN THE KITCHEN

KENA SHAH, DO

I was born in a small town in India — a country whose cultural history spans more than 4,500 years and houses the Taj Mahal, the world renowned iconic emblem of love. However, traditionally the Indian society has been a male dominated one, in which women are seen to play a role subordinate to men. Nevertheless, I was blessed to be born in a very educated and loving family and had a wonderful childhood. I was brought up with all the comforts one could ask for, received the best education, and never realized that I lived in a patriarchal society.

But, life always comes with a set of challenges. At the age of eight, I found out that my dad's coronary angiogram showed more than 95 percent blockage in five of his major arteries. He was recommended an urgent bypass surgery at the young age of thirty-three. The news came as a shock to my family. The images of my mom crying at the news and the memory of my dad being wheeled out after the surgery still remain fresh and alive in my mind. Fortunately, his health improved, but the impact of this incident was so strong that I decided to pursue medicine at a very young age.

Right after I finished high school, my family decided to move to America. I was hesitant to leave my friends and relatives but was told that "America was a land of opportunities" so I decided to trust in God and take a leap of faith. When I came to America, it was an absolute culture shock for me. I had to learn everything from scratch — the language, the culture, the customs, the laws — everything. At the same time, my family started suffering from financial crisis. And hence, to help support my family, I started working odd jobs at McDonald's and Dairy Queen. My dreams of becoming a physician had taken a back seat, and I felt like I had entered a phase of depression. I had no friends in this new country and no money to call my old friends. I started keeping more and more to myself and felt like I was getting surrounded by darkness. I did not want to share my feelings with my parents because I knew how hard they worked just to meet our basic needs.

One fine morning, my parents sat me down and asked me to leave my job and start taking pre-medical courses at a university so I could start pursuing my dream of becoming a physician. Tears rolled down my face as I saw that they had picked up double shifts to pay for my tuition. It felt as if a new ray of hope had risen, and I decided to work twice as hard to make my parents proud. That year, I took 49 credit hours and ended up graduating from university in 2.5 years. When I got an acceptance letter from a medical school, I was elated and wept tears of joy. I was twenty years old and happened to be the youngest student in my class.

I graduated from medical school with honors and got into my top choice residency program. Residency was not just hard with long hours but was also emotionally challenging. I remember one specific incident. I was working nights and taking call in the ICU when I admitted an elderly white gentleman who had suffered from acute respiratory failure secondary to decompensated heart failure. I had spent the whole night by this patient's bedside. I intubated him and put him on a ventilator, started a central venous line to administer vasopressor medications to help maintain his blood pressure, and at the same time put an arterial line to monitor his vitals signs closely. His blood pressure was very fluid and I had been constantly managing him by making changes to his vasopressor medications. By the time I left in the morning, his blood pressure was adequately controlled, and his condition had stabilized. Two days later when I returned to the ICU, I learned that the patient had been successfully extubated and was doing well. I was ecstatic to hear that and decided to swing by the room of this patient who I had spent the whole night trying to save.

When I went to his room, he was sleeping comfortably so I decided not to wake him. A few hours later, I got a call from the nurse stating that the patient wanted to speak to the doctor. I went in this patient's room with my nurse, a middle-aged white man. When the patient saw me, he started directing all his questions to the nurse. The nurse kept redirecting the questions to me, but the patient wouldn't make any eye contact with me and showed displeasure on his face knowing that I was his doctor. Regardless, I made sure all his questions were thoroughly answered.

When I left the room and was charting the patient's progress, the nurse came to me and apologized on behalf of this patient's behavior and told me that after I left the room, the patient asked him if there was any appropriate white male physician in this hospital. The nurse told him that I was the one who had saved his life when he was in the most critical condition, but he didn't seem to care.

That night at 3:30am, I received a call from the same nurse telling me that patient's oxygen had started desaturating as per pulse oximetry. I had to re-intubate him, put him back on the ventilator and restart him on vasopressors. I again, spent the rest of the night making sure he got the best treatment possible. I ended my ICU rotation that night so I never got a chance to see the patient again. I was happy to find out later that he did well and was discharged home. When I met the nurse again, he informed me that he had told the patient that I had saved his life for a second time. The patient, however, didn't care because I was not only a "colored" individual but also a woman, and "women belonged at home." It hurt, but I decided not to wallow in it. I was proud of myself for doing my job right and for saving a man's life, regardless of his opinion about me.

Right after the intense ICU rotation, my husband and I decided to take a vacation to Universal Studios. We decided to take our relatives as well since they were visiting from India and had never been to Orlando. They were vegetarians, and because vegetarian food options are usually not as abundant, we decided to pack some home cooked food for them. When we sat down for lunch that day, they opened the bag only to find out that we had forgotten the food at home since we left in a rush.

"Oh, Oh," I said, "How did we all forget?"

To which I was told, "It's not 'we', this is a girl's job to remember to pack food."

Well, I kept quiet and swallowed my words since I was always taught to not "speak back to elders." But that was a second stab to my heart in a very short period.

ॐ

I WENT ON TO FINISH MY RESIDENCY WHILE APPLYING FOR a fellowship in allergy and immunology. At the time, there were only four osteopathic allergy and immunology spots in the whole country. I was overjoyed when I found out that I had got one of those four spots! When I happily shared the news with my family, however, I got a response quite opposite of what I had expected. The fellowship was across the country, and I was advised by all my close family members, that I should take whatever job I could that was close to my husband's job and be happy. They believed because "I was a girl I shouldn't move away from my husband even if it was for further education." I was shattered.

My husband asked me that night, "If you were to listen to the rest of the family and turn this down, will you regret this decision in five years?" And without a blink of an eye, my answer was "Yes." However, I felt powerless as it was me against everybody. Hence, I had decided to turn down this wonderful opportunity. But, my husband spoke on my behalf the next day and convinced the rest of the family that even though we would be in a long-distance relationship for two years, our bond would only grow stronger, and that he completely supported me. He felt that I should be allowed to follow my dreams. With mixed feelings, I moved across the country to start a new life, but I couldn't be happier to have a husband who supported me when I couldn't stand up for myself.

Time flew by, and it was the holiday season. I woke up early on a Wednesday morning to see all the hospital consults before I flew back home for Thanksgiving. I was the first one to arrive, and the rest of the family members were going to fly in the next morning. My mom and dad had just gotten home from work. Despite having a long day, mom quickly entered the kitchen to get dinner ready for all of us. Meanwhile, Dad watched TV, waiting for dinner to be served. Mom talked about how her job had been extremely stressful over the last few months and taking care of the kitchen along with work had become more and more challenging for her. Hence, I casually asked my dad why he wouldn't help mom out with the daily dinner preparations. To which my dad very sternly replied, "Cooking is a girl's job. It's time even you start learning how to manage the kitchen."

"Cooking is a girl's job."

Those words seemed to echo in my head for the next few minutes. I was in disbelief; I just couldn't believe what I had heard. Did these words really come out of my dad? MY dad? My dad who took on two jobs so I could go to medical school and achieve my goal of becoming a physician? My dad who gave me the most wonderful childhood I could have asked for? My dad who had proudly raised two girls, two girls who turned out to have very successful careers because of his upbringing? Did he really believe that? No, maybe I didn't hear him right.

But then he continued on to say, "We should have raised you in India. There you would have learned what your true responsibilities are."

Within seconds, my eyes filled up with tears of disbelief, and I felt like I was choking on my saliva. I couldn't hold back my tears. I wasn't just crying; within seconds I was bawling.

I looked up at my mom and said, "I want to go back home, my home."

To which my mom, who was also still processing the conversation said, "This is your home! Finish your food, and we will continue this talk after dinner."

I tried to eat, but I couldn't and had to leave to clear my head.

All of a sudden, my whole life sort of flashed in front of me. I realized that I had decided to ignore what I had seen my whole life. Mom and Dad go to work at the same time every morning and come back home at the same time every evening, but after coming home, Mom was responsible for the kitchen while Dad waited for dinner to be served. This I witnessed every day of my life. How did I not see this? Or did I see this but just unconsciously decided to ignore it? What I realized was that when I am in the context of a daughter, I am given the best of everything — all I am required to do is study, play, and enjoy. But when that same daughter is in the context of a wife, I am required to cook for my man. It doesn't matter if I'm at the top of my career or not. It only mattered that "I am a woman." I cried myself to sleep for many nights but then eventually started some soul searching, and I learned some of the most valuable lessons of my life.

1. **BELIEVE IN YOURSELF.** DON'T EXPECT APPROVAL OF yourself from anyone. Don't let anyone's one sentence lift your spirits because if you do, their one sentence can also bring you down. You cannot control anyone's behavior or perception. But yes, you can control your own mind and find a way to respond to situations.

2. **PRACTICE MINDFULNESS.** ANGER IS A SIGN OF weakness. Your mind is powerful. You need to learn to create the right thoughts. Meditation and a daily dose of spiritual knowledge gives you the power to be at the receiving end of unkind behavior and still maintain your integral qualities — which are love, peace and purity.

3. **FORGIVENESS IS THE KEY TO REMAIN HAPPY.** WHEN you forgive people, you are not doing them a favor; you are helping yourself move on. When you let it go from your mind, that's liberation, that's freedom, that's emancipation. Remember — no one can hurt you, your mind has a lot of power, and no one has the power to hurt you but you.

4. **LEARN TO FACE THE SITUATION.** KILL THEM WITH success; bury them with a smile. Facing a situation means not to hit back, magnify, or to blame. Accept the situation and then learn to resolve it with constructive criticism.

5. AND FINALLY, **AIM FOR THE SKY.** DON'T LET YOUR failures or hardships define you; let them refine you. Nothing in this world is impossible because the word impossible itself means I'M Possible.

11

SLOW DOWN AND HEAL

BANDE VIRGIL, MD

"ETA 4-5 minutes we need all providers and nurses
ready."
"Does anyone know what the story is?"
"MVC of some sort with unknown number of
restrained passengers, some ejected."
"Child patient, school aged found down and
unresponsive, CPR in progress"...we could hear
over the transmitter.

That's the usual conversation that happens as the synchronized symphony of the busy ER begins to receive multiple traumas. The trauma bay was ready to receive each patient: the full count of injuries was uncertain. Some of us paced, others began quiet prayer, but we were all ready. There is never any warm up. Unlike a dancer or athlete, you don't stretch and then begin the full sprint in this line of work. On certain days, you pull up into the parking lot, gather your supplies for the day, finish the last drop of your coffee, and then get out. As you walk onto the floors of the hospital, overhead the paging mechanisms are already indicating that there is distress in the world. People can be injured, become sick, or even approach death at any given moment. You have an immediate response to action. Sometimes you join those who have already been laboring through the day or night as their relief yet no one clocks out. We hang in together until the case before us is resolved; sometimes meaning that ten hours of work becomes twelve, or twelve becomes fourteen — particularly for physicians. Unlike other members of the medical team, we don't clock in and out; there is no overtime pay.

Looking around my immediate space, faces of many different disciplines reflected back at me including people that I knew well along with others I was meeting for the first time in this critical moment. I suppose this is how all first responders feel in a moment of crisis. The Who and the What matter little; the team comes together through the magic of our common language.

The patient rolled in, and we all assumed our roles: head of the bed for airway, chest compressions, IV line access, pharmacy, team leader. This was not a drill. Counting chest compressions, time stood still for me. In my ears I could hear the count of respirations as another provider used the bag. Our patients color was not improving, his dusky skin tone remained; the pulse remained thready and difficult to obtain. The vitals on the monitor remained bleak. Epinephrine, a vital medication for resuscitating a patient, was called out, and then another dose.

In the aftermath of those moments, we all stood in silence. For what felt like the entire morning, but in reality was a reasonable sequence of minutes that we had all been trained to execute, we had done all we could. The air literally deflated out of the room, and despite our best efforts, there was nothing more that could be done. The child was gone.

I imagine that just a few hours ago this child woke up this

morning, had breakfast with family members, brushed his teeth, and got dressed. He may have watched some TV or perhaps played with siblings. Today was not a school day so perhaps the family was planning to run an errand or groceries at the store. If this child was lucky, they were off to do something fun like roller skating or bowling. Who knows what adventure this day held for the patient lying still before me? Life changes in a flash, and our plans dissipate like dust.

In pediatrics, people always ask how it feels to lose a child. I don't ever really know how to comprehensively respond to that question. We spend so much of our days in laughter at the funny things our patients say. I often walk into a room to meet a shy toddler who isn't feeling well seeking refuge in his mother's or father's armpits. I walk in and say, "Hi, I'm your doctor. Can I check on you?" My patients who are too young for pleasantries sometimes and often have absolutely no filter, will yell a resounding "nooooo!" and hide out even more. It is absolutely hilarious and adorable. The poor parents are often mortified that their child isn't compliant and easy to evaluate. I always reassure them; we get it. Pediatricians are experts at the full spectrum of children's emotions, especially sick children. There is never a need to apologize for an anxious toddler. WE get it. Sometimes my patients are filled with curiosity, and we spend the first few minutes getting to know each other. They examine my stethoscope by using it on a doll, stuffed animal, my arm, or their parent's chest. Those are good days. That's when I know there is still a spirit of strength inside there.

There are other occasions when a child lies listless. You can literally raise an arm, and it will flop back onto the stretcher without any resistance or strength. Touching the stomach of the unresponsive child won't illicit a giggle or a movement away.

Does this get easier? No. It never does.

In the hallway outside of the trauma bay, we could hear the wailing of several women. Apparently this young patient's mother had finally arrived. Her cries echoed throughout the space around us as they bounced off the ceiling and the walls, shaking all of our spirits. I felt my legs fail me; my throat was parched, dry, and unable to get any relief from my own saliva. First a whisper and then a voice that I didn't recognize spoke out as we all started to make eye contact. We began to coordinate the tasks at hand: finishing the assessment, talking to the mother, and finding out the story.

One of the great things about the specialty of pediatrics is that we don't do this alone. Police, social workers, a chaplain, and the nursing staff — we all carry this difficult load together. As this mother voiced her grief, and she collapsed in the hallway at the news of her child being gone, the chaplain and social worker team came to her side. She was gently guided into a private waiting area as several of us joined her. How do you explain to a mother that her child is dead? How do you even process this with a father or grandparent? In the typical sequence of life, a child is supposed to outlive the parent. That is the natural order of life. We see this cycle turned upside down in the work we do. Each time is different as each family and situation are a unique tapestry; it never gets easier. It never should. For me, that is the beauty of the human experience as a pediatrician. I celebrate with my families at the amazing victories of overcoming illness, recovering from horrible accidents or unpredictable twists and turns in their lives. I am also there to hold a hand, offer a prayer and give a hug, or stand in respectful silence with my families. The patients are the children, but the entire family is under my care. A child should never function outside of a unit; adults are the surrogates for decision making.

"We did the very best we could."

"Unfortunately your child has passed away."

What is the best way to say this? Every time I had to hear or say these words, it felt awkward and strange. Is it better to be blunt and say *"your child has died"* or a bit vague and say, *"your child did not make it"*? Each person processes death differently. There is no correct way. We must constantly honor the life that was lost and operate with the highest level of compassion.

"I just went to work...all I did was go to work," said the now deceased child's mother.

"They were supposed to be watching him. Now he's gone...just like that."

The sobbing again took over. The story was coming together. The family members trusted, loved, and adored this child. They had been left to care for him like they had done on many other occasions except this time there was a fatal accident.

Losing a child is the worst nightmare of most parents. We spend our time hovering and watching closely as our infants grow into toddlers then school aged children and further into the teen years. Most parents, myself included, are careful about who cares for their children. We split hairs about it and even spend sleepless nights deciding on who we should entrust with our most precious gift. A loving family is a blessing to working parents. Under their watchful care our children flourish; they are stand-ins for parents. The reality is that accidents can and do happen at any time even under the watchful eyes of loving extended family. These same accidents can happen in the midst of loving parents. Life is unpredictable, and despite our best efforts, death can come. How could I explain this to a grieving mother? Thoughts flashed of my own children and I realized there was no adequate consolation; just working through the emotions.

We spent time reassuring the mother whose natural response was guilt. Guilt is probably the most common denominator in the scenarios when a child is lost. Working parents feel guilty they were not there in the last moments. If they had been there, perhaps this could have gone differently; maybe the child would still be alive. Guilt seems to be one of the most universal reactions experienced by parents who lose a child in an accident. They replay in their mind every scenario. "If I had just stayed home..." "If he or she had just gone to a different place..." "If..."

Once we finished talking with this mother, additional support staff continued to sit with her. As I passed the room where we had just concluded the unsuccessful resuscitation, it remained uncleaned. For the first time, I looked at the wrist of my white coat to see the splattering of blood that had gone beyond the gloves I was wearing. I took my coat off and began transitioning to the rest of the duties of the day.

And, just like that, I moved from the organized chaos of trying to save a life to the systematic duties of the rest of my patient care day. I knocked on the next patient room, straightened up my scrubs, and readjusted the badge on my ID. I took a deep breath and formed a relaxed and welcoming smile on my face.

"Good afternoon, I'm Dr. Virgil..."

I think most families do not realize that physicians do not get a lot of time to process the grief and loss of patients. I suppose at the end of a shift it's possible when you end up wrapping up your notes and heading out of the hospital. However, if there is a trauma or rapid response called for a patient whose condition may become life-threatening done in the middle of the shift or day, or even first thing in the morning, you must still complete all the work of the day. In some cases, more of the same may even occur. You have to quickly recalibrate and be ready for the next case set before you.

So, when encountering a pediatrician who seems to be a bit guarded or exhausted, take into consideration that they may have been taking care of dying children the entire day; all day seeing the reflection of her own children in each patient with little time to process.

Hours into a day of work or shift, perhaps with a quick break to eat lunch, that day, like so many others, finally came to an end. I used the time driving home from work to listen to gospel music and soothing sounds of R&B to relieve the tension in my shoulders and the stress pressure in my chest from the day. On days like this, it is nice to have a commute; having time to transition from work to home. I could not imagine walking out of the hospital and straight into my home to immediately address the new set of demands from family: homework, attention, preparing meals, catching up on the day. My family is such a blessing, but on days of this particular level of intensity, where there has been literally no time to myself, the alone time is fresh manna to my soul.

Driving, I thought back on the resuscitation and processed different scenarios. Could the outcome have been different if this had happened, or that had been done — but the final outcome is always the same. Nothing could change this. Today this was God's will. Yet before I knew it, I began feeling tears slowly fall, my vision became cloudy leading me to pull over recognizing that I needed a moment to collect myself. Just a moment, in the car alone, I sobbed, once again crying for the life that was lost today.

So how is it that pediatricians like me survive when young patients die?

The hierarchy of medicine doesn't give the physician room to openly experience mourning and sadness. It is often just not acceptable in our medical culture. We are the leaders, the stabilizing forces, the ones who have the answers. While our staff gather to debrief perhaps with a chaplain or other administrative staff, many of us must continue on our clinical duties just as I did that day. There is often no one to cover us while we process these losses; we don't get a scheduled break time. Our staff looks to us for emotional support, yet we infrequently receive that support in reciprocity.

All life is precious, and I don't mean to undermine the difficulty of adult losses on my colleagues who practice adult medicine. However, there is something unnatural when it comes to the order of life in a child's passing. We think often about all the things he or she never experienced or accomplished. In some instances, life is snuffed out even before it has really begun. If you have ever attended a funeral for a small child, you know this pain. There is so much to the story of that life that will never be written. As a mother myself, I struggle with not allowing these cases to turn me into a helicopter parent.

As pediatricians, we survive like all who mourn loss and deal with dying though many people believe that pediatricians are stronger, super humans built of mortar and stone. This is so far from the truth. We survive through the support network that holds us together. We are mothers; we are members of families; we are human. Due to HIPAA constraints, we are not able to vent to people who were not involved in the patient's case so the details of the loss are often not shared, but the emotional support of our spouses, siblings, and close friends is invaluable. This is how we survive.

After time to myself to process this type of difficult day, I walked into my home and said to my husband, "Today was tough. We lost a young child today, and it was extremely sad."

Fortunately for me, our friendship and love is such that I don't have to elaborate any more than that for him to understand. It doesn't require a physician's degree for him to show compassion and empathy. He treated me with a hug and offered to take care of a few things on my to-do list so I could have some more time to mourn. He asked me if I wanted to talk more about it as I stood in his arms and simply cried. You see, for me, tears are therapeutic. It is a way of purging pent up emotions that would otherwise stifle me and become overwhelming. I found relief and then calm in this final release of emotion.

Dealing with hard days like this one push me to find solace in my faith. Knowing that God has the final say in all things gives me peace. My faith fortifies me in my calling as a physician. God has equipped me with the ability to help Him save lives. However, despite all my valiant efforts, I am not God. There is peace for me in this reality. The ultimate decision about life is not mine to make. I work and work diligently until my work is done. Yet that particular patient remained with me.

For several weeks on random nights, I woke up with the memory of his grossly deformed face in my mind. I am sure this was nothing compared to the mourning his family must have endured. Even only knowing the patient for a few minutes, as his physician I carry this lost patient with me. Lots of other physicians do this too. After the families leave and the day is over, most don't remember that we are more than just practitioners. As human beings carrying such heavy weight can be difficult requiring ways to find healing or a healthy way to cope. In order to be functional, physicians have to seek healing for all the trauma we see and take care of. I am more than a doctor; I am a mother, daughter, wife, sister, and friend. I encourage other doctors to slow down the moments and find time to heal themselves from the trauma we see.

12

BE AN OVERCOMER

DANIELLE J. JOHNSON, MD, FAPA

Y ou would think that someone who knew she wanted to be a physician since she was in pre-school would have had an easy road to becoming one. Well, think again. When I was in pre-school, I told my older brother that I wanted to be a doctor, and he said I had to be a nurse because girls couldn't be doctors. My older brother got on my nerves at the time so I was determined to prove him wrong. I continued to have plans to be a physician but had other careers in mind that probably crossed the minds of many teenage girls: ballerina, author, fashion designer, model, singer, etc. However, those were all fantasies to me. My reality always came back to medicine.

In my childhood mind, I wanted to be a physician to "help people." As I grew older, I understood it was a fascination of how the human body worked and having the knowledge to maintain health and treat disease. I was a straight A and honor roll student until my senior year of high school when I didn't feel like working as hard. That year I didn't mind getting a B. I still graduated with honors and received a full scholarship to college because I was a National Achievement Scholar. But after most of my childhood wanting to be a physician, what did I decide to do when I went to college? I majored in physical therapy. I could not see myself spending four years in college then going to medical school for another four years. I was also not ready to incur the cost of a medical education. I chose physical therapy because it was a steadily growing field and would still satisfy my love of anatomy.

As I went through college, I continued to do well and eventually figured out that being a physical therapist would not make me happy. It was not until the end of my sophomore year that I decided I had to pursue medicine. I was watching an episode of "20/20" in my dorm that showed the story of a patient whose Parkinson's disease symptoms were resolved after having a brain surgery. It brought me to tears. Although I was not certain if neurosurgery was the field for me, it reinforced how life-changing and amazing the field of medicine could be.

So now I had a dilemma. Could I change my major altogether knowing now that I wanted to be a doctor and not a physical therapist? The only major that would not cause me to lose credits and fulfill the prerequisites I needed for medical school was Exercise Science. I was supposed to do an internship with clinical work, but I chose not to because I knew I would never work in the field. I eventually graduated with a Bachelor's of Science in Exercise Science, a degree I would never use.

Since I was late in the pre-med game, I was behind in the Medical College Admissions Test (MCAT) and medical school application cycle. I took a job as an office assistant in a neurology office while I studied for the MCAT and applied to medical school. Remember earlier, when I mentioned I was a good student? I thought I was such a good student that I only lightweight studied for the MCAT and did not do well. I still applied and got accepted into one school. It was a 5-year program for medical students who were designated as disadvantaged applicants. My application was not strong because I didn't study, not because I was disadvantaged so I did not want to take the spot from a student who qualified for it. This gave me more energy to push even harder to go to medical school on my own terms. I continued to work, really studied this time, took the MCAT again and performed much better. Thankfully my hard work paid off, and I was accepted and enrolled in an MD/MPH program. I ended up not pursuing the MPH because I felt the program was disorganized.

The most difficult transition for me was realizing that although I was among the smartest in high school and college, everyone in medical school was too. I soon realized in that setting, I was average. I have never had to work so hard at anything in my life leading to just average results. Many times I felt like my classmates were having more fun than me. While they had the time to socialize and enjoy the city our medical school was in, I was studying. Another stressor, although I did not see it that way at the time, was my relationship. My college boyfriend and I became long-distance when I went to medical school. He actually asked me to withdraw from school and come back home and re-apply to medical school at the same time he planned to start law school so we would be in the same place. It was tough. I would be on an Amtrak over half a day to visit him. Eventually, he moved to where I was but hated it and frequently let me know. That was the beginning of the end of our relationship.

With all that going through my mind, I got through the first two years of being in the classroom and taking exam after exam. Getting to clinical rotations in third year was a breath of fresh air. Finally, this was what I came to med school for, to take care of patients − not memorize the Kreb cycle. However, my third-year bliss was quickly interrupted by my reality of finding out that I failed the United States Medical Licensing Examination (USMLE) Step 1. I was allowed to complete my current rotation but could not start my next rotation until I retook and passed Step 1.

I studied so hard during that time off, took the exam, and...failed again by one point! I was sad, angry, disappointed, frustrated, and hurt. Truthfully, I felt stupid. I questioned whether I was intelligent enough and had what it took to be a physician. I even contemplated quitting. Then reality hit that I already had six-figure student loan debt. I had to try again because I needed a career that would give me a chance to pay the loans back one day.

I enrolled in a live test prep course in New York City. I was away from my boyfriend, stalled in my medical school career while my classmates were moving forward, and had to spend money on the course and living expenses. My time there was not as bad as I thought. I had the experience of living in Queens with a roommate from a different culture, connecting with my brother and some of his friends since he used to live in New York, sightseeing, going to Broadway shows, and eating amazing food. And guess what? I finally passed the test and did very well. I would not be able to graduate with my class, but I was still on my way to becoming a physician. I was not the only one who was in this position. Several people in my class failed Step 1 so I was not alone. I realized that maybe it was not us, there might have been some deficits in our training.

During this trying time, a Bible verse gave me strength, and it is still my favorite verse today: John 16:33, "I have told you these things so that in me you may have peace. In this world you will have trouble. But take heart! I have overcome the world."

When I returned back on my clinical rotations, it opened

a new world of possibilities for me. I went to medical school with the intent of becoming a surgeon. I was also considering neurology as I previously worked in a neurologist office and because my mother has multiple sclerosis. As I went through my rotations, it was very easy for me to determine what I did not like.

With the exception of when I actually got to participate in surgeries, I hated every minute of my surgical rotation. I liked to talk to patients, and I spent too much time talking to them when I just needed to do a wound check. I was not made for surgery. Obstetrics and gynecology was another to cross off — again, due to miserable residents. Possibly, I would have felt differently if those rotations would've happened at different hospitals with different residents and attendings. However, I am glad I did not enjoy them as it led me to where I am now.

One rotation I really liked was family medicine because of the option to see patients in the hospital or in clinic, do procedures, have knowledge about multiple specialties, and develop a relationship with patients of all ages. I initially planned to apply for a family medicine residency. Then I received my evaluations for my psychiatry rotation and received the highest score of honors after performing excellently on my psychiatry exam. I never considered psychiatry but reflected on why I did so well. I realized that I enjoyed my psychiatry rotation, and the patients I liked and connected with most in all of my rotations were those with a mental health issue.

I was still hesitant and somewhat confused on what to choose for my career. At that time, I felt there was less "medicine" in psychiatry, and people wouldn't consider me to be a "real" physician. Even some family members didn't understand that a psychiatrist was a physician. I kept thinking of my maternal grandmother who had multiple health issues and was planning on me graduating medical school and being able to take care of her. When I told her I chose psychiatry, she was offended and felt either I wouldn't be able to take care of her or that I thought she was "crazy" based on my specialty choice. I also realized how difficult my medical school journey had been and how I needed to make sure I was doing what I loved. I felt I had a talent for psychiatry, and it was a career that many medical students didn't want. If I enjoyed and had the ability to connect with the patients that no one else wanted to even have a conversation with, I had an obligation to do it. The concern from my family and friends about my choice of specialty reiterated the stigma of mental health in the black community. Psychiatry needed someone who looked like me. I truly believe it is what God wanted me to do.

I passed USMLE Step 2 with flying colors. I was still concerned about having to explain my Step 1 failures to residency programs, but thankfully it did not hinder me as I matched with my first-choice residency. As I mentioned before, I would not be graduating with my class. I did not have to complete an entire extra year of schooling, but there are no winter graduations in med school. So, I completed my remaining rotations and moved back home until graduation. During this time, I was able to let my family love on me, reconnect with friends, and truly realize how much God had done for me (He overcame the world!) I continued to try to repair my relationship with my boyfriend, but our relationship remained long-distance as I once again moved away for residency. We attempted to make it work, but it ended about two months afterwards. Thankfully, the stress of this didn't impact my ability to perform and made room for new experiences.

During intern year, when I was on my medicine rotation, I took care of a woman whose family I connected with. After she was discharged, her son came back to the hospital to give her medical team thank you cards. We exchanged numbers (remember, she was not my patient anymore, and I was finished with internal medicine), started dating, and became a couple. I later became pregnant and had our son during January of my second year. My program director was late in making third-year work schedules because of accommodating my upcoming maternity leave. My co-residents were upset and wondered what was going on. I had to tell them that I was pregnant before I was ready in order to stop the speculation that someone was leaving or kicked out of the program.

Many women residents have been pregnant during residency, but there are some special challenges with being pregnant during a psychiatry residency. I was working with psychotic and manic patients who could potentially have delusional thoughts about pregnancy. Some psychiatric patients in the inpatient and emergency settings could become violent. I was not going to put myself or my baby at risk so I could not participate in de-escalation or restraints. This led to additional work for my colleagues. Because of the fatigue of my pregnancy, I did the necessary work but did not go above and beyond. So this meant no research, volunteering, or grand rounds. I did well, but flew below the radar at the same time. The demands of being a new mother also didn't allow for me to do anything that would enhance my curriculum vitae. But I did continue to grow and excel...and easily passed Step 3, my specialty boards, and was able to graduate from residency.

Even though my application did not stand out when it came time to apply for my first attending position, I got job offers everywhere I interviewed. I had to seek out an interview with my own residency program, which was embarrassing and humbling. Although I am an introvert and have performance anxiety, I was able to interview well and was offered a position. I also interviewed at a new private psychiatric facility that was affiliated with my department. I did not think I had a chance to get the job as two of the top researchers in my department and in the field of psychiatry would be the chief executive officer and chief research officer. Again, I interviewed well and was surprisingly offered a position. I accepted as I wanted to be part of something new, different, and innovative.

When I first started working at my new job, I was nervous and worried I would not measure up. I was the only physician in my department who was fresh out of residency, and once again I found myself in a situation where I was behind my peers. I soon realized that I had what it took to be an attending and was very good at it. I had confirmation that not quitting was the right decision, and that God placed me in this field.

Since that time I have been vice president of the medical staff, president of the medical staff, and am now Chief of Adult Psychiatry. I have served on the board of my local National Alliance on Mental Illness (NAMI) chapter and on multiple committees of my state's Psychiatric Physicians Association. I was also honored to be chosen as a fellow of the American Psychiatric Association (APA), an organization of psychiatrists working together to ensure humane care and effective treatment for all persons with mental illness. The strength I developed during my difficult journey to become a physician prepared me for many challenges I would face years later and helped me continue to strive in adversity.

13

I THINK I CAN

PEAESHA L. HOUSTON, DO, MS

Ambition

As I lay in the dark in our small one room home where each living area was delicately separated and sequestered by long thick sheets and curtains, I knew that tonight would be like most other nights had been. I would either be dragged away from my peaceful and naive slumber by the sounds of screaming and violence or be curiously awakened by the cries of silence which would tantalizingly engulf the room. Tonight, violence was chosen to be the victor.

I awoke in the twilight hours to find my father and mother fighting on our small living room floor. Fits of terror and anger swept over me as I noticed that he was violently yanking the hair from my mother's head with a pair of large rusty old pliers. Although I was only around eight or nine at the time, I thought I was invincible. My spirit had not yet been broken so I anxiously, yet fruitlessly, attempted to destroy my father's hold on my mother. I was immediately thrown to the floor. As I lay in the corner watching and hoping that the violence would end so that I could comfort my mother, I soon began to cry myself into sleep.

This was the beginning of the debilitated mentality I inflicted upon myself. From that moment on, and for many years thereafter, I felt helpless in life. Even though I myself was never abused, I was still a child living at the whims of angry men hoping that bruises and beatings would not happen to my mother today. My inability to save my mother from both my father's abuse and later abuse she would receive from other men, made a certain ambiguous resentment for my mother grow and simmer like something cooking on an old wooden stove. I questioned, "Would this too be my lot in life?"

It was not easy growing up as a child, and being poor didn't make it any easier. Living with an un-providing and absentee father left my mother and me with nights of agonizing hunger and loneliness. And so, after years of subservience, violence, and infidelity, my mother finally found the strength to leave my father behind. So, with no job and no real home of our own, "off to grandparents' house we went."

My grandmother Beth and my grandfather who we referred to as "Didy" lived on the outskirts of our town in an old white wooden home with green trimming around the roof and large fields of cotton as far as the eye could see grew to the north, east, and west. In the summers when the cotton would bloom, it looked as though we were surrounded by blankets of white crisp snow. It was like a winter wonderland but without the winter's freezing chill.

They were poor people, my grandparents, and they knew it. Their home never had running water, and most of their food was grown in the small, crude garden outside. But what they did have, we were unquestionably welcomed to.

I was a happy and wild child for the time I lived at my

grandparents' home. Long, hot summer days were filled with climbing and swinging from tree to tree as if I were an orangutan in a South American jungle. Cool, peaceful evenings were reserved for exploration. I would roam around searching for things in the loose black soil as if I were an archaeologist trying to uncover the origins of the human race.

There at my grandparents' home, where I had finally found my sanctuary, I created my own little private world, usually away from the companionship of others. I would often hide away behind our torn and worn out furniture. Behind the dust and the darkness was my place. In this world I created I could be whomever I chose: an astronaut, a lawyer, or even a doctor.

Good things don't always last, however. Soon the ravages of disease would invade my family as it eventually does to all. As is the circle of life, my didy that I so cherished was not so special as to escape its grasps.

That year was the very first time I ever saw snow, and as we searched through it that freezing, winter morning, I was overcome by fear and frustration. Where could he be? What if he was hurt, or worse, what if he was dead? Freezing weather was no place for an 80 year old man with Alzheimer's disease and dementia to be; especially when all he was wearing was his plaid colored pajamas and slippers.

Although we did eventually find my grandfather that day at the police station wrapped in old jail cell blankets, following one of his many breaks from reality and descents into madness; the many experiences like this my family and I had with him, left a lasting impression on me. As he continued to struggle with and eventually lose his fight with Alzheimer's, it ignited in me a desire to know the nature of disease and to have a better understanding of the human body. I became fascinated with all things medical. Why did people have to suffer and die from such diseases like my grandfather did, and how could they be treated and possibly cured? I dreamed of being the first in my family to get a college degree, and even greater, the first in my family to leave our small town and follow my dreams.

Self-Doubt

But who was I to dream so big? I was a small town nobody from a place in Louisiana that was one of the last strongholds against desegregation; a black girl living where a clear divide between the haves and have nots was permeate and obvious; where eye contact was evaded and inferiority complexes persisted. "Yes sa" and "no sa" was still a part of the standard dialect in my parts.

Although at that time, becoming a doctor seemed like an insurmountable feat, I decided to pursue it head on.

"I think I can, I think I can, I think I can!"

I would be a natural. I'd be able to stop bleeding in a flash and insert IV's at the click of a wrist!

But where to start. Why even try? Luckily in this journey of life, we are never alone no matter how godforsaken it may seem. Encouragements, pushes from others, and a small fire inside me that even the most hopeless of situations could not extinguish continued to fuel my journey.

Fear

One step was behind me now. After much persuasion from a beloved guidance counselor, I attended and eventually became a college graduate! Throughout college and beyond, my passion for medicine continued to grow. I immersed myself into various scientific research positions such as working with the National Institutes of Health (NIH), researching the avian flu, and working as a microbiologist. I had come this far, but questioned if I was really capable of being a D-O-C-T-O-R; a title that to me garnered prestige, intelligence, and immense responsibility. It consumed me! I chose the road of inaction. I gave up. "This is too much to bear. Too much to take on. I cannot do this." I was in the 10th round of a heavyweight fight with my opponent backed in a corner and instead of a knock out, I took off my boxing gloves and threw in the towel.

Rejection

For years a sense of longing and incompleteness followed me like a dark cloud; it overshadowed all my accomplishments. I knew that if I did not pursue my passion for medicine, it would forever linger. I would always wonder "what if". So I applied! And...rejection 1, rejection 2, and rejection 3 soon followed!

"Hey, just because you want to be a doctor doesn't mean you can; it's not cut out for everyone. Why are you torturing yourself?" those close to me would say. Despite the naysayers, something inside me would not allow surrender. I thought long and hard about what would make me a better candidate. How could I prove my worthiness? I decided to pursue an advanced degree in biology and ultimately completed a master's degree. I would try again.

I don't know if it was my tenacity, my exceptional performance during graduate school, or the sheer annoyance of seeing me apply and interview year after year, but the moment I heard the admissions coordinator over the phone say the words "you're in," it didn't matter!

Acceptance

In two weeks I would be getting married; in three weeks

I'd be starting medical school; and in four weeks I will have probably lost my mind, I thought. I was ready to leave my "Grey's Anatomy" fantasies behind and delve into the real world of medicine. There'd probably be no "McDreamies" or "McSteamies" in the average med student's life. This was my calm before the storm. (I envisioned medical school as a storm, but it was more like a Class 4 hurricane.) In the weeks and months before medical school started, I resisted the overwhelming urge to study and instead savored the sweet victory of my acceptance into osteopathic medical school. I was pretty lucky — almost 40,000 applicants apply each year and only about 18,000 are accepted into medical school.

Failing and Struggle

As my medical school orientation approached in T-minus one day, not knowing what to expect and venturing into such unknown territory, I began to quiver in my boots. But, as Helen Keller said, "Difficulties increase the nearer we approach the goal...From a certain point onward there is no longer any turning back." So, I welcomed the unfamiliar and braced myself for the weeks, months, and years ahead.

A sense of surreality enveloped me as I walked through the tall, heavy, wooden doors of the anatomy lab for the first time as the lines from my favorite movie, "Gross Anatomy", which I'd watched a hundred times, began to play in my head, and my anticipation grew.

"Look to your left, look to your right, one of you will not be here at the end..."

I hoped I would not be that "one". As the administration and faculty addressed us, they discussed how privileged we were to be there. They stressed the sacrifices our patients for the next year had made. Once vibrant and alive, their now lifeless cadavers appeared frail before us. Each body was painstakingly encased in wrapping to preserve their delicate and intricate anatomy awaiting exploration by the eager learner. They had gifted their bodies to the art of medicine and science in the final hopes that we would be better physicians because of it and that our future patients would reap the rewards from their deaths and of our training — one last gift from the dying to the world.

All of the doubt, reservations, and loneliness I felt suddenly melted away. This was no place for fears and insecurities! I was in the big leagues. We were students from around the world, rich and poor, Ivy League and state, all pursuing the same goal to one day be a doctor. I was now playing a game of survivor, and my goal was to "outwit - outplay - outlast"...well maybe not the outwit and outplay part.

"I think I can! I think I can! I think I can!"

That first year was the most difficult of my life! Although for some reason I did frequently hear the occasional, "You are making this look so easy," it was far from easy. Only a select few were trusted to see my fits of crying, complaining, and self loathing. Eighteen hour study binges reigned. Five minute nap breaks turned into four hour blocks of sleep from pure exhaustion. This was followed by frantic awakenings with the realization that precious study time had been lost. Were these smushy convoluted things called brains I studied for hours on the anatomy table meant to hold so much information? Or was it my will that needed the work out?

My first anatomy exam was like a nightmare, except I was awake! Everything seemed unfamiliar as I walked to each station to identify the structure marked with a dangling white placement card. Did the body miraculously grow new parts I had never seen or heard of before? I felt like Dorothy in Oz — foreign and afraid. I wondered how I would recover from such a huge fail. I tried harder. I studied harder. Eighteen hours increased to twenty hours. I asked for help. I had not come this far to fail and to be sent home after decades of struggle, sacrifice, and perseverance.

Triumph

Something began to change. My studying became more efficient and less like a ravenous cheetah trying to devour her victim before the opportunistic hyena tries to steal her meal. I survived gross anatomy — the hardest, most challenging course of medical training. Then, I survived the first year. Soon I began to not only survive but thrive. I went from barely passing to excelling. I watched as some quit and others failed, but somehow I survived. I, who was no more capable or prepared than my colleagues who'd lost this war with the time-eating, life-consuming monster that is med school.

Mahatma Gandhi once said, "Man often becomes what he believes himself to be. If I keep on saying to myself that I cannot do a certain thing, it is possible that I may end by really becoming incapable of doing it. On the contrary, if I have the belief that I can do it, I shall surely acquire the capacity to do it even if I may not have it at the beginning." I believed in myself. I persevered. I thought I could, and I did.

❧ 14 ❧

WHEN MENTORSHIP MATTERS

ALANA BIGGERS, MD, MPH, FACP

"I won...I won the award?!" I said to myself during my last days in residency. Though exciting, the journey to getting there is where my story begins, all of it tied to my up and down relationship with Impostor Syndrome.

Impostor Syndrome is a concept I did not learn about until my first year of residency but had experienced years prior to knowing what it was. I remember the first day I heard the term as I was watching the comedian Tina Fey. I was listening to a clip from her book Bossypants and heard her explain Impostor Syndrome in an interesting way. I understood the sentiment as soon as I heard her say, "The beauty of the Impostor Syndrome is you vacillate between extreme egomania and a complete feeling of, 'I'm a fraud! Oh God, they're on to me! I'm a fraud!' So you just try to ride the egomania when it comes and enjoy it then slide through the idea of fraud." She was describing me! I nervously laughed when I heard the term and how she described it. And in that moment, I felt that someone understood me. I was not alone in my feelings. Like her, at times I felt like a fraud.

Unfortunately once I heard about Impostor Syndrome, I

realized that it probably plagued most of my adult life starting from my experience when I applied to medical school. Getting into medical school was not an easy task and is likely where I first felt feelings of 'do I belong.' It took three tries before I had an application that was worthy of any medical school admission offices taking notice of me. When I finally was accepted to medical school, I was delighted but still felt that I did not belong. I remember during our white coat ceremony one of the deans said to my class that we can stop worrying about not getting into medical school and that this dream of being a doctor was real. Needless to say with my Impostor Syndrome, I still held onto the admission letter anyway. Fortunately, the Impostor Syndrome has not stopped me from progressing forward, learning my craft, or trying new things. I was able to successfully finish medical school and enter internal medicine residency. But every once in a while, the thoughts of being a fraud still would creep into my head. Residency was no exception, and the lack of career mentorship while I was there for three years made matters worse.

Residency training felt like an experience in isolation for me at times as a black female doctor. As most people know, medicine is still a male dominated field. If I think about it, most industries are male dominated. Even though 2017 marked the first time that more women were enrolled in medical school than men, according to the Association of American Medical Colleges (AAMC), in my specialty, internal medicine, today about 63% of the physicians are male and less than 6% of trainees are black. My residency program was no exception and was without diversity.

Though most of my experiences and the people I worked with were great, there were some interactions that definitely fed into my Impostor Syndrome. I survived and did well in residency, but often, I did not feel supported. While I was a resident, I was assigned to three different faculty advisors. Before I could get to know one advisor, he or she left, and I was then assigned to another leading to me never receiving consistent advice or support. Keep in mind that mentorship is usually one of the keys to successful progression through residency. It also helps to know someone has your back. But not having that made me feel even more isolated and that I had to defend myself and my reputation. This came in full effect after a work incident with a superior.

At the end of my second year in residency, I challenged an attending's ability to break an admission rule regarding a 'problematic' patient who was recently discharged from his team and was supposed to be readmitted under his care. My team and I did not mind having another patient but felt this abuse of power was wrong, and being the senior resident, I spoke up about it. His breaking the rule would benefit his team but not mine. I was my team's protector, and I took my role to heart. Ultimately, this attending won because, of course, he was the attending! Unfortunately, the event did not blow over well as he began to characterize me as 'difficult to work with' which added a negative view to my previously unflawed reputation. I was devastated. To have previously won three awards for working well with the nurses and now be deemed as being difficult? It was a designation that shattered my confidence, and often times brought back thoughts of the Impostor Syndrome to mind. How dare this attending label me that way when I work hard to take great care of patients and work well with my colleagues?

Thankfully, I felt like I had some support from most people including my co-residents. We bonded over tough times in the hospital with baked goods, Costco and Trader Joe snacks, and lots of laughs. Not letting that one instance hold me down, I still had wonderful experiences and worked on teams with other residents treating lots of patients. We all worked well together. I also found that during this tough time my first two advisors were very good, even though our relationships did not last long. For my third year, I was assigned to another new faculty advisor...the same attending I challenged previously; the one who broke the admission rule. I wanted more support from him as my mentor, but because of our previous interaction I never felt fully supported.

Our relationship was cordial but never fully blossomed to the supportive relationship other residents had with their advisors. I only met with this advisor a few times throughout the academic year. Each time our interactions felt forced. Each time I cringed going to his office and often felt justified for my feelings after I left. My work ethic and my ability to work well with healthcare teams was questioned many times despite having only positive outcomes and overall good work reviews from attendings and co-residents. My advisor just made the situation uncomfortable for me. I received minimal advice including important topics that should be discussed with every resident like studying for boards or applying for jobs after residency.

Even though feeling unsupported, I kept moving forward. These incidents motivated me to be a better resident and ultimately a better person. I worked hard to maintain great relationships with patients and worked well with surrounding health teams. When I was the senior resident on the team, I continued to protect those who worked under me from misuse or abuse as much as I could. During the last few months of my training, my mind began to move past residency. I started to dream of the day I could take the best and worst of what I learned to become a great physician for my patients. With all the bad, does come some good.

Not all of my interactions were poor. I had an amazing outpatient clinic supervising doctor who showed me how a caring physician should conduct herself professionally. Additionally, I met a research mentor suggested to me by my first advisor who helped to shape my current career path.

With my background in public health, I wanted to conduct research with a mentor who had similar interests. I have always had an interest in health disparity research and was able to develop a project under my mentor's grant during my last year in residency. My job was to analyze a dataset of women over 65 with breast cancer and look at how the Extra Help Program (federal program to help people with Medicare and Medicaid pay for medications) assisted with their persistence and adherence of hormonal therapies. Doing this research was the first time I felt like I had purpose in my program.

At the beginning of my third year, I had a month to work even more on my research. With the help of the statistician, I began writing code to better analyze the dataset, something I hadn't done in years. The statistician handled the advanced statistics. Overall, it turned out to be a great project. After my that month, I continued my research by going in the office on nights and weekends to finalize the analysis.

Over the course of my last year in residency, my confidence grew after every interaction with my research mentor and clinic supervising doctor. When people asked me what I was working on, I was able to explain the project and the analysis. Finally, I found a place I could excel and felt I was good at something without being judged negatively. And surprisingly (to me), everyone had similar reactions to my new found skills as a researcher, skills that I thought other residents had too. Actually, I felt very behind my peers because I waited until my last year of residency to do research. I thought my co-residents were also doing data analysis because so many of my colleagues were presenting at conferences and discussing their research. I assumed that included literature reviews and data analysis, but I soon learned that this was not the case.

My research mentor was great! She was busy but kept pushing me forward. She also encouraged me to submit a research abstract on my current breast cancer project to a national conference which she helped edit and gave me more direction. And with her guidance, the abstract was not only accepted but also became one of the featured abstracts for the conference which usually does not happen for resident research projects.

As the end of my third year came to a close, I finally found my stride again and felt more encouraged. Despite the awkward encounters with my unsupportive advisor, I managed to have two great mentors. I applied for jobs broadly and received a faculty position in academic medicine where I would teach medical students and residents in training. My unsupportive advisor was shocked I wanted to stay in academia and provided minimal career advice...which wasn't a surprise to me. My research and clinic mentors were the ones who gave me career advice; they suggested I stay at my residency program and build a career there. Mentally I knew I could not stay. I knew it would be a battle to fit in as an attending. But their advice gave me insight on the types of jobs to look for and how to negotiate my salary.

FEELING MORE ENCOURAGED AS THE END OF RESIDENCY drew near, I did the unthinkable...well at least I could not have imagined doing this in my first or second year...I nominated myself for the residency research award. This award was given out to four residents per department each year.

While I was filling out the form, I laughed to myself because I knew I was not getting the research award. Other residents were presenting at conferences, and I did not even attend any conferences until the end of residency. In addition, my program director had to decide which nominations to submit. Since I was designated as a 'difficult' resident, I knew I was not getting picked. But then I got through the first screening and was picked as a nominee...I was pleasantly surprised. I knew there were more than four nominees so my program director had to choose, and I actually made the cut.

Four weeks later while working in the hospital, I felt a buzz followed by a buzz and then another buzz in my pocket. Realizing it was my phone, in my head I said, "What is going on? Is everything okay? Why is my cell phone buzzing so much?"

When I had a moment to myself, I saw a message. "CONGRATULATIONS!"

"Congratulations?! For what?", I thought.

Then the next message: "Congratulations. I knew they would pick you for the award. You deserve it."

Wait...what? I won... I won the award?!

Third message... "Congratulations, Alana, on your research award."

I could not believe it! I signed onto my email to read what my friends were already telling me...I was one of four recipients of the residency research award. My program director and the selection committee thought that my research was noteworthy. At that moment, the struggles, the awkward encounters, and emotional drain were worth the sacrifice. I accomplished something that defied what I previously thought about myself — thoughts of me as an imposter, a fraud. At that moment I realized that the biggest obstacle I faced was dealing with my feelings of 'not belonging.' When I thought everyone was ahead of me with research, I found out that was not true. I also discovered that by finding an area that I was interested in became the key to my success in research. After all, I did not involve myself with just any project. I found the right project I felt passionate about that could contribute to science. I realized in that moment, though it took many years, that I was and am no imposter. I was happy for the award and proud of myself. I felt that my hard work was finally paying off. I also recognized the opportunities placed in front of me. Despite not receiving the best advice overall, I received a connection from my first advisor which led to me meeting my research mentor.

Sometimes feelings of Impostor Syndrome still pop in my head. I am now an early career physician at an academic institution. Being at the beginning of my career, everyone really seems further along than me. But then I remember residency and know it is not how you start but how you finish. I was able to finish strong in residency despite obstacles. And now I have a supportive mentoring system in place to help in my progression. I am not an imposter. I am a great physician and a budding researcher. I BELONG.

15

FINDING MY PLACE

AMBER ROBINS, MD, MBA

T aking that first step out of my beloved silver Rav4 SUV and walking onto the campus of my new school as a medical student, I remember not knowing what to expect. I traveled thousands of miles from Louisiana to upstate New York for the opportunity of becoming a doctor. I was proud of myself for even making it this far in my professional aspirations as I did not have any doctors in my family. I figured that I could be the first with others to soon follow in my path, hoping that their journey would be easier than mine.

I have to admit that at that time I thought medical school wouldn't be that hard. I breezed through both high school and college without much difficulty. I was at the top of my class and was known as the "smart girl". But little did I know that when I walked into the room with my new medical school classmates, I would be one of many smart people. It was a reality of which I would constantly be reminded. My class of a little more than 100 people included only fifteen black medical students. Coming from a historically black college and university, this was a stark difference for me. I automatically felt that I did not easily belong. Later I realized that I wasn't the only one with this struggle.

The first semester of my first year of medical school, I remember my best friend telling me she overheard one of our Jewish classmates talking about another peer. This classmate said a fellow black student must've been enrolled in medical school due to affirmative action because there was no way she was good enough to be a doctor. Hearing that statement made me think. Why would she say that? Were people saying the same about me? I knew my grades weren't the best, but I was still able to keep up with my class. In that moment, I began to see that people were watching the minority students very closely. Because I happened to be one of them, that meant they were watching me too. I put extra pressure on myself to do well in my classes and push forward to at least be an average medical student; below average was not an option.

Keeping these facts in the back of my mind didn't help though. I added additional stress trying to study even harder while not reaping the rewards. My grades were still mediocre. Plus, I began to see that I didn't really fit into the box of what I thought a doctor should be. At my medical school we didn't have many doctors of color and didn't learn much about diseases that affected people who looked like me. Plus, I kept having the recurring thought that where I grew up in my predominantly black community, I didn't see many doctors of color either. This caused me to wonder if people who look like me even belonged in medicine.

I remember one day as I sat in the auditorium near my best friend, who just happened to be at the top of the class. We were learning about skin disorders in our dermatology section. I nudged her and asked, "Have you noticed that all the pictures they've shown us so far in class have been of white people?" She thought about it and then nodded her head "yes." I told her that I found that interesting because I knew I would be treating people of color yet I was getting little to no education on how to do it. What an eye opening experience for me. So, not only did I feel left out because I am black, some of my future patients were being left out as well.

Throughout medical school, I had many experiences like that. With my frustrations and just my determination to survive medical school, I was desperate to find a place where I felt I belonged. I know that if I couldn't do this, I wouldn't be able to finish the hardest level of schooling I had ever experienced.

One day as I was waiting to talk to one of the few black administrators at my medical school, I saw a magazine that was hanging on the wall. It had a beautiful drawing of a black woman surrounded by the colors of yellow and gold. The title of the magazine was "The Journal of Minority Medical Students." I grabbed the magazine to show it to my adminis-trator and asked if I could take it. She said yes and as she did I quickly put it in my backpack to read later.

When I looked through the magazine later that day inter-ested in what I would find, I saw a page that was asking for medical students to submit articles to be published. I thought to myself, "Maybe I could do that. Maybe this would at least help me use the medical knowledge I have acquired over my first year of schooling in a unique way. Plus, it would be amazing to be published in a magazine where people look like me." So I did it. Little did I know that in that instant, I began the journey of finding my real place in medicine.

After contacting the editor of the magazine by email, I was asked to have a phone conversation with her. I was excited, but figured that I would likely only be asked to write an article or two. Apparently, I was dead wrong. By the end of my conversation with the editor, I was asked to write a column called "Diary of a Medical Student" which would be about my experiences as a minority medical student. I couldn't believe it. I began to write article after article while still making mediocre grades in medical school, yet I started to notice that I was having more fun. Unknowingly, as I was budding into a medical doctor, I was growing into a writer as well. By the time I finished medical school, I had over a dozen articles posted in the magazine all while experiencing the grueling days and nights as a "struggling" medical student.

⚜

At the end of my fourth year, I matched into a family medicine residency program which I was somewhat excited about. The part that made me unsettled was that I would be starting residency in Wilkes-Barre which was in rural Pennsylvania. I knew that there I would really be one of the few black faces. I still tried to be as optimistic as possible and decided to take one of my mentor's advice. He told me to keep writing and document my time in Pennsylvania by blogging. He thought people would be interested in hearing about a black female doctor in a predominantly white rural city in Pennsylvania. I agreed that it was an interesting story and figured that just like writing got me through medical school, maybe it would get me through residency too.

Residency in rural Pennsylvania was quite interesting to say the least. In the hospital, I actually began to feel I belonged because surprisingly I had three black attendings who I worked with several times during my intern year. It was the first time I had worked with so many black doctors ever during my time in medicine. One was a hospital adminis-trator who talked to me about his administrative job in the healthcare system while we performed C-sections together. The other two questioned why I was in family medicine and even offered to write letters of recommendation for me to transfer into Ob-Gyn residency since I was so good at it. Of course I was flattered but declined. Working with those doctors was amazing! They made me feel that being a doctor was something I could excel at, even as a black woman. I felt at home in the hospital, but when I stepped outside, it was a different story.

When I first moved to Wilkes-Barre, I began my search to find a church as a way to tap into the black community. The search was brief since there were only a few black churches in the city. I went to one of the "bigger" churches with a congregation of a little over 100 people. After the church service, I talked with the pastor who spoke great things about the church, but the good things stopped as he told me about the city. Simply put, he said that the best way to describe the city was to say that it was stuck in the 1960s. For me, hearing that made me afraid. The 1960s was not a decade that I would like to relive or repeat. Although African Americans made great strides during that decade, racism was very rampant. Residency was hard enough to handle; now on top of that I had to deal with overt racism as well.

I began to see more of what the pastor meant as I spent time in Wilkes-Barre. First thing in the morning, I looked out my window at a confederate flag proudly raised outside my neighbor's house across the street. I also began to notice that my white neighbors would watch me go in and out of my house dissecting my every move. Close to the end of my intern year, I even was racially profiled by a police officer who followed me as I was driving in my car for about five blocks only to tell me that I didn't stop at a stop sign about a mile or two back. Although I began to love the hospital in which I was working, I didn't like the feeling the city was giving me. I had to escape.

I began to reach out to as many people as I could to switch residency programs. I even considered changing specialties and almost applied to an anesthesia residency. I contacted my medical school on what to do next as I had never heard of a resident switching programs before. Then something interesting happened. As I was contacting the program director in the family medicine program affiliated with my medical school in Rochester, it was the same week that one of their interns dropped out of their residency program. (Look at God!) It appeared like I could be returning to Rochester, NY. Shortly afterward, I interviewed there and by the time the interview day was over I pretty much knew I had gotten the job. I returned to rural Pennsylvania to complete the rest of my intern year relieved I had found a way of escape. Even though I found a spot in a place I was more familiar, I knew that I still needed to find my place in medicine. I began to look back to writing as a way to guide my search. It led me to do something I had wanted to do for years. During my last rotation in my intern year, I began to write my first book.

I was on my ICU rotation in Wilkes-Barre at that time and began finding ways to cope with leaving my residency program while handling the pressures of taking care of very sick patients. Although for many residents working in the ICU is the worst and hardest month, for me it was the most defining time of my medical career. I began to think about all the articles in my column that I had written during my medical school years and wanted to reconfigure them in a new way. I don't know where it came from, but I had a brilliant idea to pair some of my articles with bible scriptures and journal entries that could be helpful to not only medical students but all people who were in a state of transition in their lives. I would call it "The Write Prescription." I talked to the nurses and some of my attendings who worked with me in the ICU about me developing a book. All of them thought it was a great idea. For me, my desire to write the book was not enough; I also surprisingly began to venture into learning more about the business side of medicine.

After having several chemoradition treatments for lung cancer and now back at work, my ICU attending who was young, in his mid-thirties, encouraged me to pursue an MBA. He told me that if I wanted to do something, do it now because it's hard to predict what life has in store whether it be good or bad. Working with him, in addition to two other doctors who were hospital administrators, led me to apply for an MBA. That same month while working in the ICU I applied and was accepted into an online MBA program.

My intern year was over, and I returned to Rochester, just a year after I first left, to start my second year of residency. During that time I felt I finally had a better sense of my place in medicine. I discovered I had an even stronger interest in writing than I first thought and had a newfound passion for business, both of which I wanted to continue to develop. I began expanding my writing skills to now focus on medical topics. One of my attendings at my new residency program pushed me to take things further. She talked to me about doing medical segments for the local news and felt that I would be good at it. Simply put...when she said this, I was like, "WHAT!?!?" I was slightly interested and mostly terrified of that proposition. However, I trusted her judgement and tagged along.

When I went to the studio at the local news station, I did not know what to expect. I kept rehearsing my topic for the day which happened to be on oral health. I thought, "Shouldn't they have a dentist here for that?" Well, by that time it was too late. I was sitting in the chair across from the news anchor with bright lights and two cameras in my face. Whether or not I felt I was the right person for the job or not, I was the person in the seat for the interview who needed to perform. In a little over three minutes, the segment was done. Then that feeling came again. The feeling similar to when I first started writing while I was in medical school. The feeling that I belonged. This was it! I began to see my place in medicine as a doctor who reported on medical topics in the media. Later, I found the proper name for such a career and interest. I was becoming a medical journalist.

Seeing my strong interest and talent for communicating in the media, my program's residency director pushed me to do even more. He strongly suggested that I do a one-month rotation at ABC News headquarters in NYC. I applied, got a spot, and went. There I was at the pulse of health news, sitting beside other medical residents who were members of the medical unit at ABC for that month. We reported on hot topics like the Zika virus and the Olympics along with reading dozens of research studies looking for interesting topics people should know about. I met many people who I had only seen on TV. People like Dr. Richard Besser and Robin Roberts, both role models for me on Good Morning America. I learned how to write scripts for health news topics that would be reported on throughout the US. What an amazing experience!

Once I returned to my residency program, I found that I had more confidence in what kind of doctor I wanted to become. It was no longer a mystery to me. Being on the news I could inspire more girls who look like me to one day become a doctor. Plus, I could talk to patients all over the world by reporting on need to know information about their health. All this could be done through media. After years of searching, I was happy to say that I FINALLY found my place in medicine as a doctor and journalist.

16

ONE NIGHT ON OB/GYN

KENDRA SEGURA, MD, MPH, FACOG

"We need a resident to room 4, stat!" were the words being yelled down the hallway, but there was no resident physician around. One resident had driven to the wrong hospital that morning, and we were waiting for him to arrive. The other Ob/Gyn resident was still in the operating room finishing up a surgery. This information was relayed to the yelling nurse by the other nurses. No doctors available. I wondered how the nurses were going to handle this. *This should be interesting...*

I watched all of this unfold while sitting behind the desk of the nursing station with study material open in front of me. As a medical student, we learned to always have study material with us —Pocket Medicine, lecture notes— anything that would fit into our white coats. The hours were long and the schedule heavy, but minced into those long, hard hours were many short periods of waiting — waiting for the chance to learn, to observe, and, if lucky, to assist. On rotations shadowing attending and resident physicians, the primary objective of the medical student wasn't to learn; it was to not be in the way. If in any situation you were likely going to be more in-the-way than useful, you were told to wait. We all fought hard to be deemed useful by studying hard and paying attention. We were like dogs begging for treats, hoping our doctor masters would throw us a bone — a surgical case to observe, the chance to assist in a central line placement; anything to get us the experience and approval we needed so that one day we might be the ones handing out doggy treats. But, no matter how hard we tried, we were still often told to wait — 10 minutes here, 20 minutes there; it all added up to hours of precious studying time. Hence, we always had something in our white coats to read; and on this particular night, a couple of weeks into my Ob/Gyn rotation, I was again reading my pocket material for I had been told for the thousandth time, as a medical student, to wait. But nobody had told the baby to wait.

"Hey, you. You're a medical student, right?"

Huh? The one that had been yelling was looking at me.

"Uh, yeah…"

"Quick, get in there!" she began yelling again. "The baby's coming!"

Wait, what!

"Hurry up! C'mon!" yelled the nurse, who I will affectionately call Old Yeller. I stood up and followed her reflexively, spurred on by the urgency in her voice, but a few steps in reasoning and self-preservation began to kick in. Reasoning reminded me that I'd never delivered a baby before and didn't really know how. Self-preservation made me regret getting up and following her as I thought of everybody watching me fumble around, and me slowly dying from embarrassment.

"I've never delivered a baby before!" I yelled in a panicked state. It was true; I really had never delivered one before. I had only observed a couple of deliveries at that point in my career.

Old Yeller stopped and turned towards me. "Don't worry,

I'll be right there with you. It's easy. Just don't drop the baby."

That's what I'm worried about!!

"But...why don't you just deliver it and...and I'll assist you!" I offered pleadingly.

"Nope. Can't. I'm a nurse. I can't deliver. Only doctors, residents, and medical students can. C'mon!"

So, we went, and too quickly we arrived at the site of my doom. Waiting for us was a woman in lithotomy position, legs and mouth wide open, screaming at the top of her lungs. I felt like doing the same, except with my legs closed, fully clothed, and even louder.

Why is this happening to me!

There are many medical students out there who have dreamed for years to be the one delivering, to have the honor and privilege of bringing life into this world. Not me. I wasn't one of those who aspired to be an Ob/Gyn doctor. When I was young, I dreamed of being a professional tennis player. I was pretty good. I got a full scholarship for college tennis. I had a good chance of going pro too. When my tennis dreams were shattered by health issues and injuries, I stumbled around for a few years doing the proverbial soul searching. I was utterly lost without tennis. I would never love again. When I finally decided to pursue medicine, I didn't aspire to be THE PHYSICIAN FOR WOMEN (with superhero cape and all). I just simply wanted a final challenge to help me find myself, to help me settle down, to work hard, have a rewarding job, live my life, and finally put tennis behind me. I wasn't 100% sure what I wanted (Infectious Disease most likely) but I definitely didn't dream of running around a big hospital system taking care of women in need. In fact, I wanted to avoid contact with women's genitals and wombs if at all possible. I could barely manage my own. I wondered who in their right mind would dedicate their life to a specialty that had you looking at vaginas all day. Not just regular vaginas, but vaginas in need of medical attention, with all kinds of sights and smells...

So that was the me who entered medical school — a vagina-averse, ex-tennis player. That was the same me standing in front of this poor woman who was in the hospital bed screaming like a banshee. The poor banshee was welcoming me with her legs wide open, and she had a wet, round, gross-looking present for me right in the middle. The wet, round, gross something was the baby's head crowning.

"Quick, gloves!" said Old Yeller, and she showed me how to don the surgical gloves as sterilely as possible. Then she practically had to shove me to the foot of the bed because my legs had suddenly forgotten how to be legs and were acting more like lead weights. She then stood right beside me and gave me quick, concise instructions, just loud enough for me to hear in the midst of all the wailing. And then it was on. A dreaded match between me and inevitability that I couldn't forfeit. With my heart threatening to pump its way out of my throat, and with hands shaking faster than any jazz hands I'd ever seen, I reached the wet, warm mass waiting in front of me. No "Hello", no formal introduction, no following of proper etiquette, but I don't think anybody gave a *beep*.

"WHY IS THIS HAPPENING!" wailed mother banshee.

That's my line!

I looked at Old Yeller for reassurance, sort of... but more for confirmation, incredulous of what I'd just heard.

"She's just in pain," said Old Yeller, confirming and explaining at the same time. "This is her fifth child...she knows what's going on...the pain makes her say stuff."

"Why!..." moaned the banshee.

See what I mean? said Old Yeller with her eyes.

Because you had sex! I answered the woman resentfully in my head.

In the midst of all the controlled chaos, nature had been steadily continuing its work of producing new life, completely unaffected by all our petty concerns, and my hands had been receiving this new life on autopilot. I looked down to see the incomplete form of what I was starting to recognize as a miniature human being.

"Don't drop the baby!" reminded Old Yeller in a quiet but razor sharp tone that cut through the din.

I readied my hands, and, when the final push came, I caught the warm, slippery nine-pound trophy with a strong tennis grip. I stared down at this warm, wet glob of life, and time stopped for a second. I was in awe.

Then out came the cord, and I triumphantly presented the complete package to the father. He had been by the bedside the whole time, holding his wife's hand, supporting quietly. It was finally his turn to shine.

"No, thanks."

What!!!

"I've done it four times already. This is our fifth child. You go ahead," he said with a smile.

I was shocked for a second. I guess I had expected the father to be gushing incessantly with gratitude when I presented my hard-won trophy to him. But his smile and tone of voice were sincere, and, the fact was, I actually did want to cut the cord. He must have seen that.

I proceeded to cut the cord (with instructions from Old Yeller). I then handed the baby, free of its life-giving bonds, to the tired but waiting mother. She smiled at me and lightly touched my arm.

"Thank you," she said hoarsely, this beautiful life-giving woman.

I think I muttered "Okay," but inside I was quivering with

suppressed jubilation. What a rush! The adrenaline! The conquering of fear! The victory! Best of all, the Zen-like noth-ingness when it was just me and the ball — that warm, wet ball of life...that moment in time when your head is totally in the game, and nothing else in the world matters...that rapturous state of nothingness! I'd never experienced anything like that before in my whole life! Except for...

A final gross, wet mass exited the birth canal, and with the placenta out, my job was complete. I had done it! I had delivered my first baby! Well, actually it was more like Old Yeller delivered the baby through me (God bless nurses; they can never receive enough thanks and credit), and the mother had done most of the hard work. But, whatever! My hands had welcomed the baby into this world! Who knew a gross, warm, wet glob could give such a thrill! But I had made a promise to avoid all that stuff after this rotation...all that grossness, a woman's vagina and the stuff coming out of it.

When I started my clerkship, I had decided that Ob/Gyn would be my least favorite rotation for reasons I've already discussed in some fashion. I decided I was just going to grit my teeth and get through this horrible mandatory rotation so that I could graduate. I promised to reward myself with as little vaginal exams as possible if I got through medical school, and that was still the case tonight...right?

The family members who had been waiting anxiously outside began to file in. There was much celebration. There was hugging, and there were tears of joy. The cameras came out. It was time for me to go. I remembered my primary objective: Don't be in the way. I began to shuffle out.

Before I could reach the doorway, I heard, "Hey, come back here!"

Huh? Me?

I turned around.

"Yeah, you!" the father answered my silent question. "Get over here! Get in the photo!"

I was ushered by jubilant family members closest to the doorway, and I was plopped right in the middle of a family photo. Old Yeller was already in position. She was obviously used to all of this. I looked at the camera, and the jubilance that had been bubbling inside me was finally allowed to come out and plaster a huge grin onto my face. Then I got hugs from everyone: big, happy, strong hugs from father and family members, and a small but genuine hug from the mother. They all thanked me for God knows what. Then the father passed the baby to me, and I held that beautiful trophy amidst all the cheering and celebration from joyful spectators.

Okay, fine. I'll give Ob/Gyn a chance.

❧ 17 ❧

SCRATCH THAT

DANIELLE LOMBARDI, DDS

"**I**f you don't have this surgery, your daughters will grow up without a mother." This line changed my family's life, and at the same time led me down a winding road to discover my true purpose. Growing up, there was a period of time when my mother was always very sick. She was constantly at various doctors trying to figure out what was wrong with her. I would often tag along at my mother's appointments, and would just sit observing the importance of the doctor-patient relationship. My mother's doctors were absolutely amazing. They were able to properly diagnose and treat her, allowing her to live her best life for many years to come. This inspired me, and I felt that being in medicine was something I could be really good at, too.

When high school came around, I was required to complete a certain number of community service hours each year. I began volunteering in a hospital where I was assigned to the surgical department. The floor was filled with many fearful patients who were either being prepared for surgery or recovering from a recent procedure. I would deliver patients meals and spend time talking with them. Having had the experience of being there for my mother, I was able to comfort many of my patients and keep their minds at ease. However, something was still missing for me. I realized that medicine wasn't the best fit. I didn't enjoy the hospital setting, yet I still wanted a way that I could build relationships with patients over a number of years.

Around the same time, my mother began working for an orthodontist, and I would often stop by after school to visit her. Initially, I would hide in the back office and work on assignments or study, but I became curious and soon began wandering around the office. The orthodontist was a really funny guy; he was always having fun and joking around with his patients. It was the intimate relationship with patients I was looking for in a fast-paced environment that I enjoyed. He allowed me to shadow him, and I began assisting the other staff as much as I could. I fell in love with dentistry during my sophomore year of high school and never looked back.

During my college years, I expanded my knowledge about the dental profession by shadowing various doctors and completing as many internships as possible. I later applied and was accepted to several dental schools. Well aware of the years ahead of me, I began dental school at NYU with the mindset to complete my four years, become a general dentist, and get out. The thought of being in school for so many years was daunting as I watched many close friends start careers, get married, and have families of their own. Of course, nothing ever goes as planned.

My mindset changed as a third year dental student when I participated in the Henry Schein Cares Global Student Outreach Program. The program is designed to send dental students, residents, and faculty to an underserved community to provide comprehensive dental care for the population. I was chosen to go to Machias, Maine, part of the second largest unprotected border in the United States. It's a very small community where the people who live there have to travel about two hours to get to the nearest dentist. On our first day, I was assigned to rotate through pediatric dentistry. This was not a popular rotation among many of the dental students, but I agreed and wanted to go where ever I was most needed. We treated over one hundred children that day; it was so chaotic yet exciting at the same time. At the end of the day when I should have been exhausted, I found myself energized and inspired. I requested to spend more time rotating through pediatric dentistry.

Even though we treated countless children during our time in Machias, one seven year old boy stood out to me. He was living with his grandmother because, unfortunately, his parents succumbed to drug addiction, something that was common in that community. Like many, this patient hadn't been to a dentist in years. He needed treatment on almost all of his teeth, but was very anxious about how it was going to be done. I saw him several times that week. Each day, we worked together to get his dental work done. Starting out frightened, by the end of the week I had gained my patient's trust, and he felt a huge sense of accomplishment. On our last day, that same previously horrified patient brought me a picture he had drawn, gave me the warmest hug, and said "Thank you! My teeth don't hurt. I can sleep, I can eat, I feel so much better." Before leaving Machias, I was convinced that I wanted to become a pediatric dentist even though I knew it meant additional years of training ahead of me. I was okay with it because I fell in love with the field. I looked forward to all the children I would be able to serve.

Previously having had no intentions of wanting to specialize, deciding to become a pediatric dentist at the end of my third year of dental school was taking a huge leap of faith. Because of the last minute change of heart, so many people told me what all boiled down to the same thing, "You're crazy. It's too late to apply. Everyone's done externships already and have been planning to apply for years. You'll never get accepted into a program like this applying at the last minute." Even after hearing this same narrative over and over again, something inside told me to apply for the pediatric dental residency anyway.

I did, however, have some of my own concerns that my past performance in dental school would keep me from my dream. I struggled academically my first two years of dental school. I was so used to school being easy for me my entire life; for years I was always the student at the top of my class, the one people came to for help. Attending dental school, things definitely changed. The first two years of dental school consisted of sitting through endless lecture hours, along with intense studying for difficult exams as well as developing clinical skills in the lab. It was an adjustment for me, and I struggled with the fact that I was no longer the straight A student I was so used to being even though I was working the hardest I ever had. My friends helped to encourage me by saying, "You can do this. Just relax and calm down, and don't be so stressed out. You know what you're doing. You're going to be fine." With their support and the guidance of my mentors, I was able to push through the first two years. Thankfully, during my third and fourth year of dental school, I really excelled as this was the time I started doing clinical work and interacting with patients.

Nevertheless, I applied to eleven programs hoping for an interview and disregarding the recommendations to not apply by some friends and faculty. All I could hope for was a program to match into. In the back of my mind loomed the facts: there's about a 10% acceptance rate for pediatric dental residency programs, and matching was very competitive. Plus, students would typically get invited for several interviews, while I was only invited for two out of the eleven I applied for. My chances of matching looked slim.

Match day came, and I nervously still remained hopeful that my dream job would be an option for me. As I opened that long awaited e-mail on Match Day, I was ecstatic to discover that I would in fact be attending a pediatric dental residency program. I ended up matching at NYU! Not only that, this was the first time NYU had matched all women in their ten positions within their pediatric dental program.

Starting residency began some of the best years of my life. While everyone had reservations about ten grown women working closely together for two years, we became the best of friends. To this day, we're always talking to each other. We're a part of each others' lives, have stood in each other's weddings, and have been present for the birth of children. Even though residency was very chaotic, having those girls there for moral support as well as just having fun made those two years of training speed by. Throughout each new rotation, OR case, studying for qualifying exams, interviewing for jobs in different states, we were each others' support system. We even had a tradition; every Monday night we would watch the show "The Bachelor" together.

❧

BECOMING A DENTIST, AND NOW A PEDIATRIC DENTIST, WAS not what I originally planned to do. I would tell my younger self, "Don't try to plan your life five, ten, fifteen, even twenty years in advance. Life will never turn out the way you want it to." Looking back, we all experience times where we doubt ourselves and are our own worst critic. During those years when I struggled in dental school, I wish I would have had more confidence in myself and knew that the finish line was attainable. Even when people would tell me I may not be able to do something, guess what? I usually ended up doing them and doing them well.

I think it was my passion for working with children that helped me finish dental school successfully and allowed doors to open up for me. I really couldn't see myself doing anything else for the rest of my life, and if I didn't get accepted into a pediatric dental residency program, I would have kept reapplying until I was accepted. Life does not come with a roadmap to victory, and our success is found within the twists and turns that we take eventually directing us to the right path. I am thankful for all of the trials and triumphs that have led me to where I am today. First, seeing the medical field with my mom and then discovering dentistry at her job helped reveal my purpose in life.

I don't think my journey is anywhere close to done. I genuinely love my career and going to work everyday. Even on the days when there are kids who cry from the time I arrive to the time I go home, my heart is so full when I walk out the door. It is an honor and a privilege that parents trust me to treat their most precious beings, their children.

❧ 18 ❧

SEASONS OF OB/GYN

KENDRA SEGURA, MD, MPH, FACOG

Part 1: Interview Season

T his was it. One click of the button, and one of the biggest decisions of my life would be made. What an anti-climactic end to all the months of gut-wrenching, hair-pulling, inner turmoil.

I looked at my rank list for the Match one more time. The list contained every residency program I had interviewed at. All the programs I had ranked at the top were Ob/Gyn; all the internal medicine and family medicine residency programs were ranked at the bottom. The way I had ranked the programs signified an intent to pursue a career in Ob/Gyn; internal and family medicine were backup plans. The magical algorithms used in the Match would take my rank list and somehow try to hook me up with the residency programs I had ranked highly. But of course, the residency programs would be ranking the candidates too so I would only get into Ob/Gyn if I was ranked highly by the Ob/Gyn programs. It's almost like being matched by a dating site. I guess that's why they call it the Match. But instead of a hot date, the outcome we were all looking forward to was a place to spend the next three to five sleep-deprived years working our tails off.

Knowing that I'm currently practicing as an obstetrician/gynecologist, you'd say it makes complete sense that I had ranked all the Ob/Gyn programs highly, but I hadn't always wanted to do Ob/Gyn. In fact, it was the last thing I thought I'd ever go into. I had planned to go into Infectious Disease at one point. I wasn't entirely certain or passionate about it, but given my time as an epidemiologist at Los Angeles Public Health, I thought it made the most sense. Pursuing a career in Infectious Disease meant I would apply to internal medicine residency and family medicine residency. That had been the plan. I had done the research, talked to people, and was ready to commit to that path. But then Ob/Gyn came along and turned my world upside down.

I didn't do my Ob/Gyn rotation till very late in my medical school career, and very close to the residency application deadline. I had left it until as late as I could, much like a child might leave their veggies on the plate till the very end. I hated the idea of specializing in vaginas. It just made no sense to me, but then I actually delivered real live babies, scrubbed in on life-saving surgeries, and saw the profound impact these vagina specialists had on people's lives. I was hooked. But, I was hooked so late in the game, and I thought maybe too late. I scrambled to assemble a curriculum vitae and application package by the residency application deadline, and I somehow scraped by with something that met all the basic requirements for Ob/Gyn. I still enacted my original plan at the same time and applied to family and internal Medicine because I knew Ob/Gyn was just some pipe dream.

Then I waited. I fully expected to get zero invitations to interview at an Ob/Gyn program. Ob/Gyn was just so competitive. To my utter surprise, I got many Ob/Gyn interviews, more than family or internal medicine in fact. To this day, I still don't completely understand how that happened. Divine intervention is my best guess. It wasn't all delight and celebration though. Interview season was tough. I had gotten many more interviews than I had expected, and not wanting to squander my good fortune, I went to every single one. I knew I'd only have a chance at Ob/Gyn if I went to all of them.

Going to numerous interviews while still trying to finish medical school was extremely difficult. I gained twenty pounds from the stress. My face blew up with pimples. There were times that I just wanted to give up. It seemed pointless anyway. The other candidates that I chatted with during the Ob/Gyn interviews boasted of well-planned medical school careers geared beautifully towards Ob/Gyn right from the start. Some would brag about how great their knot tying was because they had been practicing surgical knots since medical school began. Some even started when they were children because they had physician parents. But I, of humble parents, who had planned for Infectious Disease, had nothing to brag about.

Yet, I somehow pulled through; I went to all my interviews. But, hard times continued. After interview season came decision time, and with that came tremendous inner turmoil. Would I really go for Ob/Gyn or just stick to the safe path? Was I really passionate about Ob/Gyn, or would the novelty wear off like so many things in life? Did I even have what it takes to survive in that field of medicine, or would I get fired or eventually burn out?

Going to every interview I was invited to allowed me to postpone my decision about residency. Being indecisive was my strong suit. I spent the weeks before the Match list submission deadline in a constant state of flux. One minute I was sure that Ob/Gyn was my destiny, the next I was laughing at how absurd that notion was. I remember turning to exercise to help me de-stress, to help me get a moment's reprieve by distracting my mind, and to help me lose the twenty pounds of interview weight. I went hard with exercise because the more strenuous the exercise, the quieter my mind got. I once ran so hard on the treadmill that I couldn't move the next day; I just laid in bed snacking and sleeping.

I also embarked on unnecessary quests in order to distract myself. The most prominent example was my secret competition with an old lady at the swimming pool. When I first started exercising again after interview season, I was so out of shape that this little old lady would lap me easily with her slow steady strokes. But I wouldn't have it. I went to the pool as often as I could; and every time I went, she was there, minding her own health, doing her slow steady strokes, providing me an unwitting target to defeat. A week before the Match list was due, when I finally made up my mind about residency, I defeated that little old lady. I was so happy.

So, there I was on the day of the deadline, sitting in front of the computer, Match list ready to be sent, just needing a click of a button. There was no more turmoil by that point. Not because I had suddenly become heroically decisive, but just because I had finally worn myself out completely with the constant inner debates. I just didn't care anymore. If I was about to make the worst decision of my life, so be it. At that final step, staring at the completed Match list, I felt a tinge of panic, but just a tinge. I pushed through and clicked the mouse button.

It was done. Finally. I sighed with blissful relief, suddenly having no doubt in my mind that I had made the best decision of my life.

Part 2: Open Season

THE KNIFE WAS IN MY HAND, BUT I WANTED TO HAND IT back to the attending physician. He had handed it to me at the start of the surgical case because he wanted me to be in the pilot seat. That's really the only way to learn surgery: to do. This was my very first C-section where I was the primary surgeon and not just the assistant. It was a big sacrifice for everybody involved — for both patient and hospital staff — to allow a first-year resident, an intern, to be primary surgeon. Having a novice perform surgery meant significantly more operating room time, and more chances for something to go wrong. I endured the awkwardness of inconveniencing everybody; but when the blood started seeping out of the patient in the middle of the surgery, I thought it was high time I handed the scalpel back to the attending.

However, the attending would not take the knife back. He wanted me to finish the case. That was the only way to learn. I tried to explain to him how, in my inexperience, I might not work quick enough to stop the bleeding, or how I might injure the bladder, or cause worse bleeding by nicking an artery.

"We're surgeons," he said. "If things go wrong, we fix it."

It wasn't boastful. It was just matter-of-fact. I was in awe of that confidence, but I was not at all confident that I'd prove him right.

"You're finishing this case, Segura. You're walking out of this O.R. with a C-section under your belt," he said with finality.

"Yeah, and by the time you're finished, the patient will be able to walk out of here with you," quipped the anesthesiologist. He meant that because I was taking so long, the anesthesia would wear off by the time I was done. Anesthesiologists generally get angry when surgeons take too long, but this one was just being funny. I couldn't laugh though.

As I continued on, muddling through the case, my chief resident was standing on a step stool, as a second assist, assisting in my education. That was her duty as the chief. She piped in intermittently throughout the case with advice and tips as she retracted for me (held open the surgical opening). She was eight months pregnant and was experiencing contractions after standing for so long in the O.R., just Braxton-Hicks contractions, not true labor contractions, but they still really hurt. She kept retracting nonetheless.

These were the sorts of people I had to aspire to be. People with gracefully dexterous hands, seemingly unlimited intelligence, awe-inspiring confidence, and a ridiculously stoic sense of duty. *How the heck did I end up here???*

At that point I was only two months into my intern year of Ob/Gyn residency, but already the Match seemed like ages ago. I was ecstatic when I had gotten the letter congratulating me on being accepted into Ob/Gyn. I was very grateful that I had somehow willed myself to go to every single interview I was invited to because the residency program that I Matched with was one of the last to interview me. Now, just months later, I was already having sincere doubts about that decision I made a lifetime ago. Why did I ever think I could do Ob/Gyn?

Everybody knows residency is tough, but nobody knows exactly how tough until you actually go through it. I learned a lot about myself in residency, like: how long I could hold my urine, or how long I could go without food or water, or how much crap I could take. As an intern, we were the lowest on the totem pole, and we all know that crap rolls downhill. Interns were blamed for everything and yelled at by everybody — attendings, senior residents, nurses, patients. Admittedly, interns did tend to make mistakes, but what do you expect from someone who's new at their job?

I woke up hours before the sunrise that morning, as I often did, in order to study. I was use to being awake while people were still blissfully dreaming. But, I was living the dream, right? I stared at my surgical textbook in hopes that the words in the heavy tome would somehow imbue me with surgical skill and knowledge. Maybe today would be the day that things would finally sink in, and I would do everything right and answer all the attending's skill-testing questions correctly. Maybe today I wouldn't get yelled at.

I eyed my life-sustaining coffee machine, but decided against using it. I was already nervous about assisting (or so I thought!) in the scheduled C-section and didn't want to be jittery during the case. Besides, coffee wasn't going to make me any smarter; it could barely break through the fog of heavy sleep debt.

Residency was one big sleep deprivation experiment, and there were some funny results. Not funny at the time, but funny now. I once went home so tired that I left my keys in the front door and didn't realize till the next morning. Another time, my wallet fell out of my pocket in the parking lot while I drowsily stumbled home from another long day. Luckily, I had good people for neighbors. My wallet was returned to me intact, and nobody came into my obviously unlocked apartment while I slept naked as I often did in residency. I didn't have the energy to even decide what to sleep in so I decided to sleep in nothing. I felt sorry for myself sometimes, but I didn't know what else to do except to keep going through the dark woods. In my especially dark moments, I felt like I was a deer trapped in the woods, and it was open season.

I clenched my jaw as I reread the same paragraph of the textbook over again, trying to squeeze out whatever focus and intelligence I might have hidden inside me. By my fifth read through of the same paragraph, I realized that today would be the same as any other day; I was still going to be a dumb, useless intern, and I was going to be yelled at again. I was going to be a deer today.

But, the attending didn't yell at me. And even though it took forever, the surgery did finally end after two agonizing hours, and things went relatively smoothly. I had done it. My first C-section! I walked out of the O.R. with dry mouth and scrubs wet with sweat. I was greeted with applause as I neared the nurses station, and the chief resident joined in. The attending patted me on the back. I raised my arms triumphantly to receive the applause not caring that there was probably a huge sweat stain in my armpits. I felt great. After almost two months of doubt and despair, I finally felt the high again. It was worth it. I now knew that whenever I found myself in dark woods, all I had to do was keep walking to reach the clearing.

❧ 19 ❧

FIRST, DO NO HARM

NATASHA K. SRIRAMAN, MD, MPH, FAAP, FABM

I knew pediatric residency would be hard. I guess you can never exactly know what residency is going to be like until you're in it. I mean, I knew it was going to be diffi-cult, strenuous and rewarding all in one, and of course the long hours and sleep deprivation; you try to mentally prepare yourself, I guess. What no one could have prepared me for is the pain, suffering, and chronic conditions some of the kids endure. As a resident physician, you become immune to the cries when you give vaccines, take blood, put in an IV, or even look in their ears and throat. In a way, you get used to it because these things are helping the child by possibly preventing a future illness. But the children we take care of on the hospital floor or Pediatric Intensive Care Unit (PICU) — the chronic kids, the "frequent flyers" as we call them, with life-threatening illnesses — to watch them suffer and endure, that is the absolute hardest part of my job. The amazing part of it is how much these children endure: their strength and their spirit are truly amazing.

I started my pediatric internship on June 24th; they had

interns start a week prior to the usual July 1st date so we would be under the guidance of soon-to-be-graduating senior residents before they embarked on a new job or fellowship. There were a lot of changes in my life: married a month earlier, graduated from medical school two weeks prior, a new car so I could drive to work, and starting pediatric internship. I was assigned to 3 South; a floor that had children of all ailments with acute and chronic issues. There were no infants on this service. We were a team of four with two senior residents. We would each take overnight call every 4th night, hence beginning our 3 years of long hours and sleepless nights. Luckily, I was on a team with two friends that I had met earlier, and I hoped that while we were friends, we'd work well together.

I remember all of us sitting cramped in this tiny on-call room, some sitting on the bottom bunk, the others on a broken futon as we began our daily ritual called *signing-out*. For those who are not familiar with this, *signing-out* is just that — the process of each intern giving all the information on each patient from the night before to the intern who would take over for that following day. This occurred at least twice daily, once in the morning and the other in the evening. It also occurred mid-day for those times when a resident had to leave the hospital to see patients in their outpatient clinic. So there was a lot of time devoted to signing-out. The goal was to be efficient but extremely thorough.

My first morning as an intern, a PGY-1, I was assigned four patients. While they were on the floor, these would be my primary patients during the day. One of these patients was a seven year-old boy. Sean had a diagnosis of congenital HIV. While I didn't train in the height of the AIDS crisis, I began my training when there were many children and adolescents who contracted HIV perinatally. Unfortunately, while research was being done on medications to reduce viral load and minimize the risks to the fetus and eventually, newborn infant, many of the patients I would care for during residency had already contracted the disease from their mothers. As was the case with Sean, many of these children lost their mothers to the disease.

That day in June, Sean had already been admitted a few weeks prior. His body was suffering from the effect of congenital HIV and was admitted for continuous care and medications. Each day Sean needed his blood drawn to follow his blood counts. Since he was my patient, I was tasked with drawing his blood. To say I was terrified would be an understatement. While I drew some blood on children during my medical school clinical rotations, I had never drawn blood from an HIV positive patient. What if he moved? What if I got stuck by the needle? Well, I had no choice. I was the intern; he was my patient.

After introducing myself and telling him that I would be drawing his blood, I remember double-gloving, as I had been taught, before tying the tourniquet on his arm. Sean didn't move a muscle, probably since he was used to this daily needle prick. He was quiet, shy, and reserved. As I took care of him on a daily basis, I didn't learn too much about him. He didn't talk as much as the other patients I cared for, and sadly, during my long shifts, whether day or through the night, he rarely had any visitors. Unlike many of the other rooms where there was a parent at the bedside, Sean didn't have anyone by his side. No one was there to read to him, watch TV with him, or hold his hand during the procedures. Sadly, he almost seemed resigned with his diagnosis and with the situation.

During my last week on the 4-week long rotation, Sean's condition worsened. His breathing became more labored for which he needed to be intubated and placed on a respirator. He was transferred to the PICU for more specialized care he now required. Before he became so ill, due to his terminal condition, Sean was eligible for a request from *The Make-A-Wish Foundation*. While the child life staff coordinated these details for patients, we interns were not always aware of these requests. In fact, I found out about this *Wish* request after he became very ill and transferred to the PICU. When you hear about these foundations who grant wishes to terminally-ill children, what do these children usually get? Trips to Disney World, meeting with celebrities, etc. But this was not the case with Sean. His grand wish was a Michael Jordan #23 Chicago Bulls jersey and a pair of sunglasses. That's it, that was his wish, his final request.

I remember hearing about this, and just feeling sad, so very sad. Sad not only that Sean was ill and likely not going to get better, but sad, even mad, that he had to endure these final moments in his life all by himself. No parents, no grandparents, no family, no family friends to comfort him, to console him, to make him feel less afraid. And, when given the opportunity for an amazing gift to bring him joy, his request was so minimal.

I remember the last day I saw him. It was my last day on 3 South. I was on the floor in my scrubs and long white coat seeing all my patients and writing progress notes in each of their charts. My final shift started on a Saturday morning and would extend for 24 hours.

After a busy call of taking care of patients on the service plus admitting new patients throughout the night, I was able to complete charts and finish my *scut* list (also known as a to-do list) before handing over the patients to the intern who would be taking over for me in a few hours. After morning sign-out, I felt relief; I had just completed my first full month as an intern. I had survived the hierarchy, the long nights, the multiple procedures, and helping sick children and their families. However, I had just one more patient to see, to check on.

I walked to the other end of the hospital and entered the

PICU. I told the nurse who I was and asked about Sean. Sean was lying there, hooked up to beeping monitors, a tube in his throat with the machine helping to inflate his lungs. He looked peaceful, without pain, but small under those crisp white sterile hospital sheets. Again, he was all alone, no family, no friends there to talk to him, no one to hold his hand. I was too nervous to touch him for fear of jostling around any tubes or wires. I touched his hand lightly, but I can't remember if I said anything.

Before walking away, I placed a bag on the bed. It contained a pair of sunglasses and the #23 Michael Jordan jersey. I remember walking to the parking garage, dazed, sad, and feeling helpless. On my way home, I called my cousin who lived in New York City. I told her what happened with Sean and asked if I could come into the city to see the kids. I showered and changed quickly then drove another 30 minutes to the city. I remember picking up my nieces and driving to the park. The three of us just played; I pushed them high on the swings and just chased them around. What I remember most from that crisp Sunday afternoon, was the fresh air, their laughter, and just thinking how healthy and strong these girls were. While I was happy that I had that outlet, that opportunity to be around children after a tough weekend call, I felt sad that Sean wouldn't have the chance to grow up, succumbing to a disease that he knew nothing about — and that he endured all of that, alone.

SEAN WAS MY FIRST PATIENT TO PASS AWAY, BUT unfortunately, he wouldn't be my last. As all physicians know, part of our training is death, the death of our patients. I still get asked/told how fellow physicians could not fathom practicing pediatrics and taking care of sick kids and watching them go through pain, or even worse, death. I can't explain it, but even though it doesn't get any easier, you hope, you pray that the good that we do for these children will make them healthier and help their families cope through very traumatic and difficult times. My hope is that we make a difference, and that we heal more than the ones we lose.

20

A TRIBUTE TO MY BESTIE

MIA S. BEN, MD, FAAP

On Saturday January 27th, my life changed forever; that was the day I lost my best friend, Stella Lynn Johnson Thomas. Stella was an educator, an advocate, and one of the kindest people anyone would ever have in their lives. This is the tribute that I gave at her funeral. I prayed for strength and promised myself I would give this tribute without shedding a tear. I was successful in doing that, but as her casket rolled away, tears began to roll down my eyes.

> *"Friends are medicine for a wounded heart, and vitamins for a hopeful soul." —Steve Maraboli*

There were Thelma and Louise, Lucy and Ethel, Laverne and Shirley, Gayle and Oprah, and even Abileen and Minny... but, did you know about Mia and Stella?

Ours was a friendship of 17 years that seemed much longer. Stella was a grand lady that I thought was too good to be true who came into my life at the perfect time. I was a new physician in Opelousas, recruited by Opelousas General. I knew a few people from the area. My physician recruiter Judy Theall and others at Opelousas General, wanted to make sure that I would be comfortable and happy practicing in the city. Judy introduced me to Stella Thomas not knowing that our friendship would blossom. Well, after our first conversation that must have lasted three hours and a face to face meeting at a local restaurant called Soileau's, the deal was sealed, I knew she was my friend for life.

Stella was what I needed, a warm, mature, well grounded, witty individual. What you don't know about me and most physicians is we are "big babies!" What Stella gave me was common sense, wisdom, and people skills. In other words, Stella kept me out of trouble! I think I brought out her humorous side even more with my crazy antics! I kept her so worried with this love of football that I took it to the next level by playing in the women's professional football league. On top of that, I even gave her a godchild who she named Queen!

Stella loved Diet Cokes and Russell Stover's chocolates, and I made sure she had her fill! I even made sure she got to meet her not so secret crush, Denzel Washington. I knew that if we were in New York and watching this man on stage, I had to come up with a way to get this woman within two feet of him! When we found out that he sometimes came out after the performance to sign autographs, I told Stella we had to book it after the play to make sure we were the first in line! Stella was tired, and her knees were bothering her from all the walking we had done earlier so I offered to carry her. She gave me a look that should have frozen me in my steps. Needless to say, she didn't let me carry her.

Eventually Denzel did come out in all his glory, and my friend was closer than two feet! On the ride back to the hotel, it was me screaming, "We did it!"

All the Sunday morning catch up talks we had before church that sometimes I had to share with our mutual friend Martin, our famous Black Friday shopping shenanigans, and the Wednesday evening (except Board meeting days) talks were all our guilty pleasures and kept our friendship fresh. We were often the solutions to each other's problems.

Stella, you were the best friend I could have ever asked God for, and I am so glad that I always told you how I felt about you. You knew my love for you was never in question. You were my hero.

FAREWELL MY FRIEND
> You're leaving
> It's time for you to go
> Your friendship was a blessing
> And I will miss you so

WE SHARED SO MANY SECRETS
> You brightened up my days
> You brought me so much happiness
> With your kind and loving ways

YOU LIFTED UP MY SPIRITS
> When I was feeling blue
> No matter what was happening
> You knew just what to do

THROUGH ALL THE UPS AND DOWNS OF LIFE
> The good times and the sad
> For 17 years you were

The best friend I ever had

GOD IS HERE TO TAKE YOU HOME
   Now you and I must part
   I love you and forever
   You will live within my heart.

21

BLURRED LINES

MIA S. BEN, MD, FAAP

I t was one of those days. You know the ones. The ones when you feel useless, like there is no hope. I felt like my purpose in medicine was slipping away especially after I had been working very hard for the last four weeks making sure that all the school physicals were completed. At least 80 patients in my practice needed physicals, and most had missed their scheduled appointments. Of course, these were the very moments when I was expected to drop every-thing I was doing to accommodate those that had missed appointments because "Lil Man" had to play in the jamboree tonight or "Ray Ray" had to go to Head Start the next day!

Needless to say I was exhausted, and my brain felt like mush, but I had to push myself to complete the day. Yet my mind still began to wander anticipating the beginning of my beloved Saints football season and thinking of who would accompany me to the games this year. (Everyone who knows me is very aware that I was and still am crazy about my Saints. That year I anticipated a better season after having the previous season with seven wins and nine losses.)

As my mind kept drifting to football, the time kept

moving along too. By that time it was 3:30pm. I remember the time because my body could always sense when 3:30pm came around like an internal clock ticking away. I took a peek at my schedule and saw that after all the hard work I still had six more patients to see before 5pm. This day was on the verge of lasting forever. In addition, I also had to make a second pass at the hospital prior to heading home. I needed to focus.

I looked at the patient that was in room 6 and instantly a smile came over my face. This was one of my favorite patients; a very precocious young man full of personality. As I finished his exam and started talking to his mom about the latest happenings in town, my nurse with a look of horror on her face came running into the room with a baby in her hands. I knew something had to be terribly wrong.

"Dr. Ben, mom said she wasn't eating well today, but I just don't like the way she looks!"

I looked at the baby who appeared very sick. The baby was ashen, had bounding pulses, and in obvious distress. I immediately placed the baby on the exam table and asked the family who were there in the room for their appointment to step out. A quick assessment put my mind on fire. I had to do something quick. I was two minutes from the hospital, and I needed to get this little one stable. A jolt of energy went down my spine. We needed to get to the hospital STAT.

Amira was a two week old infant of a Muslim family who had been a part of my practice for years. In the past I would always try to make her family comfortable, especially with the current political climate of anti-Muslim sentiments. I had several Muslim families in my practice who had expressed their fears to me. Being I always gave them a soundboard, my goal was always to reassure them that everyone didn't think badly of them. I had just seen them a week ago after Amira was discharged from the NICU. Coming into this world wasn't the easiest for her. She was observed for one week for sepsis in the NICU after both her and her mother had fever at the time of her birth. Just a week ago, she appeared to be very healthy at her first newborn visit, but now it was clear that things had drastically changed. Whatever happened, it must've happened quick.

Knowing baby Amira's history, quick decisions needed to be made as she laid on the patient table getting even sicker with each second. At that moment I felt the best thing I could do was drive the infant to the hospital myself, something I have never done before. I picked up the baby and told my nurse to meet me at the hospital. Her mom was screaming and crying as we all jumped into my car.

The two minute drive seemed like hours. I kept reassuring myself that this was the right decision because waiting on an ambulance would waste more time. It would take five minutes to call and talk to the ambulance, another ten minutes for them to make it to the clinic, and an additional two to get this baby to the hospital. Each minute could mean Amira's condition would get worse. So driving her to the hospital was the only option.

As I pulled up to the hospital I was able to give a little sigh of relief that we made it safely. My pediatric nurse was waiting to assist with getting our little patient some big help as she now was having more issues with breathing. Amira was quickly rushed into a hospital room, and more medical providers came to help. We needed to get fluids into her, but because of the severity of her illness, IV access was almost impossible. Still multiple attempts had to be done until we got the IV in her. We were finally able to secure access, and as I was yelling out orders, medical personnel were feverishly obeying them hoping for the best outcome.

With such a dire scene I noticed something was different in the room. The hospital was the same. This was the same hospital that I would round on patients with during the week. I knew this place like the back of my hand, but it felt as if the atmosphere was slightly different.

As the nurses were following the orders giving life saving treatment, several of them were also praying out loud for the Lord to give us the skill to save the little one. I even began to pray out loud myself. I then looked over in the corner, and there were her parents praying in Arabic; praying to the same God as me. The spirit was moving as we assessed our weary patient, hoping for her to take a breath.

Thankfully after a few minutes, the color began to return to our little patient's body and her breathing improved. All of our interventions worked. Now we had to figure out why she got sick so quickly.

We ran blood tests, did an x-ray, and ordered an echocardiogram to look at her heart. Finally after an echocardiogram was done, I was able to tell the parents why their baby got so sick. Amira had a serious heart condition called dilated cardiomyopathy making it hard for her heart to pump blood to the rest of her body. She needed to be transferred to another facility to have more specialized care. Although grateful that we had answers, her parents were aware that things were serious and that their little girl was very sick. Her parents, with tears in their eyes, were still gracious as they thanked all the personnel for saving their baby's life. We were able to transfer the infant without incident to another facility. She was later transferred to Children's Hospital in New Orleans for further care.

After having a trying day of seeing lots of patients and doing school physicals, Amira and what happened that day stuck with me. As serious as the scene was to get her from my clinic to the hospital, there were many blessings given to all who were involved in her care. At that moment, all political views were out of the window. There were medical personnel and parents, not Christians or Muslims. Just grateful parents and elated staff sharing a moment. We did our job well that day, as medical providers and as human beings. What a day!

My mind then wandered back to my Saints who were playing at home that weekend, and I knew that I would attend the game. That weekend I was pleased when they won! Just as my mind was in a restful place, I couldn't help but think on little baby Amira in the PICU fighting to live. I just had to see her again.

Weaving through post-game traffic, I made the long journey to the place of my training, 200 Henry Clay Ave; the place where Amira was eventually transferred for a higher level of medical care. I was able to visit the baby and family in the unit. Her grandmother expressed thanks for all that I had done to stabilize the infant. Just being there was a relief and also brought back so many memories. This hospital was also very familiar to me. It was the place I trained to become a pediatrician. I was pleased at all the changes since my residency. The PICU was no longer on the first floor, but now on the sixth floor. I knew they would take good care of her there. Baby Amira was later released from the hospital after almost one month.

I still see Amira and her family in my clinic, and today she is perfectly healthy. Around Christmas her family surprised me by honoring me with a Christmas present. After that experience with my Muslim family, it just marvels me that whenever I think my work as a physician does not matter, God uses moments like this to strengthen my faith and help me to continue this journey as a physician.

❦ 22 ❦

CULTURE AS A VITAL SIGN

NATASHA K. SRIRAMAN, MD, MPH, FAAP, FABM

I was a third year medical student in Brooklyn, New York. As an Indian immigrant who moved to this country at a very young age with physician parents, I had already experienced various aspects of healthcare from different perspectives. However, growing up in rural Pennsylvania, my parents' patient population contrasted with my clerkship experiences in Brooklyn.

Here in Brooklyn the racial, economic, cultural and linguistic diversity was welcoming. Even though I was able to speak two languages, in addition to English, I didn't have the opportunity to really use that skill until I was in my OB rotation. Even 22 years later, I still remember the situation so vividly: the clinic, the staff rushing around, me standing there in my short white coat — but most importantly, the patient, a woman in a *hijab*, the traditional Muslim head covering, standing with her husband.

This woman, an immigrant from Bangladesh, who had recently arrived to this country, entered our OB safety-net clinic for her prenatal care with her husband. They quickly approached the nurse's desk and the husband began to converse with the nurse in his broken English. Out of nowhere the husband began to raise his voice in frustration with a matching appearance on his face, all telling me that something just wasn't right. I gingerly approached the couple, the woman welcoming my presence as she realized that I slightly resembled her/them.

Although we didn't speak the same language, between his English and my Hindi coupled with the cultural nuances, the situation became clearer. This woman, an older woman here in the US to have her baby, was Muslim, as evidenced by her hijab. In the religion of Islam, maintaining modesty is an overarching Islamic ethic. For observant Muslim women, covering up the body is important when they are in the company of males to whom they are not related by blood or marriage. I was somewhat aware of this since I had grown up with many Muslim family friends. However, this intersection of medical care within the context of religious beliefs was new to me and had never occurred before during my short tenure as a medical student working in a clinical setting.

On that particular day, there were only male OB residents who were seeing patients, ironically, they were of the same religion. When the husband tried to explain their concerns and religious restrictions, they were basically given an ultimatum: see the male resident or leave the clinic. And then of course, she was given the dreaded label of *The Difficult Patient.*

I tried to explain the situation to the staff, the nurses and the residents — but to no avail. In her Bengali tongue, which overlapped with my cursory Hindi, she asked me, "Can you deliver my baby?" I explained to her that I was a medical student, a doctor-in-training, and that I was unable to do so, but that I would try to help them. As they stood in the middle of the clinic during a very busy afternoon, I made my way through different staff, nurses, and doctors. Finally, my concerns were taken seriously, and I was informed that there was a midwifery service affiliated with the OB program at our hospital. After receiving this information, I sat down with the husband and wife to explain to them what a midwife was, what their role would be, and how we could transfer her OB care to the midwifery service.

To say they were grateful would be an understatement. The woman's eyes welled up with tears, and she cupped her hands in mine just saying, "Thank you" in Bengali. Her husband shook my hand and gave me thanks. From there, she went for her prenatal check-up with one of the midwives. I still remember feeling satisfied; happy that we had found a resolution so that her obstetric care would not be compromised while respecting her religious beliefs. But I also felt sadness and concern wondering if everything would work out for the couple and their baby as they navigated through our confusing and complicated medical system.

FAST FORWARD 2-3 WEEKS LATER. I WAS STILL ON MY OB rotation, but now was on the floor, the in-service unit in the hospital. Back then, there were no duty-hour restrictions, not even for medical students. Call nights usually were 24-30 hours long, but I didn't mind not one bit. I loved being in the hospital, helping mothers through one of the toughest but most exciting times of their lives. While many medical students fought to simply deliver the baby, I enjoyed the actual care of the mothers, the long hours of timing contractions, checking cervical dilatations, and monitoring blood pressures while making them comfortable during the laboring process. Of course, the nurse and obstetrician were in charge, but the benefit of training in a big city and an urban hospital was the fact that as medical students we would see a wide variety of clinical situations. Actual hands-on patient care was valuable and brought to life things we never could have learned by just reading thousands of pages of text.

It was around 9 or 10 pm, and a laboring woman was getting admitted. I looked at the name and recognized it immediately. This was the Muslim woman I had met a few weeks ago in the OB clinic! As I ran over to her room to see her, both she and her husband recognized me immediately and smiled. I guess I can imagine what it must be like to be in a foreign country, the customs, the culture, the language and then see someone, a 'doctor' who looks like you, understands your culture, and can (almost) speak to you in a language you can understand. I introduced myself to the midwife and quickly told her the story of how I knew her patient. I asked her if I could stay for the delivery, to which the midwife agreed. Within a half-hour, I had helped the patient deliver a healthy, beautiful, term baby.

To this day, this story sticks with me. Even though the mother and father thanked me, I really have so much to thank them for including what they taught me. Throughout the preclinical years in medical school, people always tell you that the real learning begins during clinical rotations. While we learn the pathophysiology of disease, memorize enzymes and pathways, and dissect cadavers to learn the orientation between bone and muscle, the true art of medicine lies in patient interaction.

This patient, a Muslim woman, taught me the value of truly listening to a patient while caring for them. We hear terms like *cultural competence* or *cultural humility*; the fact is that cultural, linguistic and religious facts directly affect health care on so many levels including health care access and ideas of wellness and healing, which can affect patient compliance. From this case, followed by so many other cases during my last two years of medical school, I realized the importance of these facets of healthcare.

Now, as an academic pediatrician, I teach both medical students and residents on a daily basis the importance of cultural beliefs as it relates to healthcare. Whether it is through lectures or direct patient care, I use what I have learned from my patients to try to educate the health team including nurses, social workers, and therapists, how culture, religion, and language can and will affect how a patient and their family receive the medical advice given to them.

The Institute of Medicine (IOM) agrees that, "racial and ethnic disparities in healthcare exist and, because they are associated with worse outcomes in many cases, are unacceptable."[9] As the world becomes more diverse, and we interact with patients from all different cultures, the awareness of these ideas will become increasingly important. As I teach my students and residents, we as physicians, cannot be expected to know every aspect of every cultural group we interact with. But, in fact, it is part of our medical exam to ASK. I have never had a patient or family get offended when asking them about certain aspects of their care/their child's care or barriers to care/medical advice and how they perceive wellness and the cause of their illness. In fact, most are relieved when they perceive that their cultural beliefs are being addressed within the medical setting.

The Bengali mother also showed me how quick we are to label certain patients as difficult based on our own inherent biases. The rapidity with which to label patients, while we may think it does no harm, actually may compromise the care of the patient. As physicians, we increasingly face more demands on our time, productivity clauses, and the rigors of the electronic medical record; it can be easy to forget to take the time to listen to our patients and allow them to tell us their story.

23

PRIDE AND PREJUDICE

NINA LUM, MD

The vice I least expected to encounter while offering the noble service of healing within the field of medicine was prejudice. For a highly humanitarian profession with the core of its substance in treating disease, improving wellness, and creating scientific ways to achieve a better life, one would expect a high level of approval from the recipients of health services. Healthcare professionals make great sacrifices as we spend a majority of our youth learning the art and science of serving mankind with medicine.

In developing countries like my country of origin, Cameroon, there is a desperate need for more healthcare providers. A means to address the increasing number of patients is necessary to close the wide physician-patient ratio there. Unfortunately, this feat currently appears far off. Inversely, with that demand comes an unspoken innate societal honor for the work performed by the healthcare provider irrespective of gender, age, race, or religion. Evidence-based knowledge reveals that the quality of healthcare delivery surpasses the act of its performance. But, standardized measures geared towards quantifying the quality of healthcare delivery is still often disregarded in Cameroon. This poses a threat to the level of trustworthiness easily imparted on doctors both in Cameroon and the US.

Apparently, neither society is ideal, but in contrast to Cameroon, over the last six years of my direct involvement in the practice of medicine here in the US, there are standardized methods in place to help measure a physician's clinical acumen and professional efficiency. There are board certifications, peer review, national physician databank reports, continuous medical education requirements, additional accreditations, and several other federally governed metrics to attain recognition of proficiency in one's field of practice. Despite the minor criticism on how accurate these methods are within the medical community, such measures make it possible for patients to identify highly skilled physicians or what some call "good doctors". But, regardless of the recognition a physician can attain for competency in their field of practice here in America, the patient can still deny delivery of service based on trivial social biases. I did not believe this until it happened to me.

I arrived at my shared physician office space one morning at 8am. With my routine in play, in preparation for the next twelve hours, I set my lunch and dinner in the refrigerator, filled up my one-liter water bottle at the fountain, and took my white coat from the rack where I left it the night before. Before stepping out the door to go to the wards, I reviewed my patient census on the document that typically sits at the front desk. These censuses are key among hospitalists; they are strictly confidential documents as they contain patient names, gender, dates of birth, location within the hospital, and pertinent laboratory data. After pre-rounding — the process where doctors check for updates from the electronic health record on each designated patient before we meet them, and they become a person again — I enthusiastically walked down the stairs from my office to the general medical floor to begin rounds.

I barely stepped out the stairwell to the floor when I could hear short fast footsteps heading toward me.

"Doctor Lum, I know you cared for this gentleman yesterday, but we will have to take Mr. Adler off your rounding list," Eunice said.

"Why is that?" I blustered.

Her typically pale skin flushed red as she bit her bottom lip while fidgeting with her fingers, and all at once she was avoiding eye contact.

"I apologize, and I am not sure how to say this, but we've had several unreasonable complaints from this patient. He stated that he did not want any foreign doctors taking care of him today, and he also made some derogatory remarks about you."

I saw a lonely streak of sweat drip down her brow as her shoulders collapsed while she released a sigh of relief. Her colleague who stood right behind her (I assume for moral support) went on to disclose how he had described me using the word "nigger" among with a slew of other profanities. At that moment, I realized that Eunice taking the role as this patient's nurse and patient advocate, was probably the most challenging thing she had to do that morning. It reminded me of another time when a nurse called to tell me that my patient had requested another doctor for no obvious reason.

Noting Eunice's concern, I displaced my angry emotions on the racial and cultural implication of what the patient said to focus on how distraught she appeared. I had a choice between showing empathy towards Eunice and creating resentment toward Mr. Adler. Despite my initial reluctance, I briefly reassured both nurses and struck through Mr. Adler's name on my list. His decision had been made, and I continued on to evaluate other patients who were interested in receiving quality care from me.

On another day on a separate wing of the hospital, I came across a pictorial used for visual cognitive testing. It was frequently used to assess the mental status and orientation of the elderly patients on that ward. It was an old print on cardboard paper that strikingly depicted the picture of a male figure in a white coat as the doctor and the female figure in a white coat as a nurse. Right after seeing this, the thought about the prior experience surfaced in my mind. The origin of unrecognized influences as it pertains to gender and racial issues in medicine, especially as perceived by the general population, began to simmer in my mind. There had been numerous scenarios where I was mistaken for the janitorial or transport staff. On one occasion, while wearing dark blue scrubs though without a white coat, I was told I looked like a representative for a biomedical device who more often than not were nurses. Due to a sturdy personal sense of identity developed through years of rigorous training, I've learned to not take offense in these role misappropriations which sometimes happen even while wearing a long white coat.

☙❧

IN MEDICAL SCHOOL THE LENGTH OF THE WHITE COAT symbolizes academic seniority. Long white coats are worn after the medical degree is officially obtained while short white coats indicate a student doctor. Irrespective of the cut and color of our coats, the prevalence of the issue of prejudice among other female and minority colleagues across the country is alarming. Biases in healthcare whether racial, cultural, age-related, or religious are far too common. They deter away from the benefit of expertise in the services being offered. I must admit that I find it interesting regarding the exposure of some of my patients.

While practicing medicine, I have had many epiphanies regarding gender especially. One I remember distinctly was when I was surrounded by medical students while teaching from a computer in a room adjacent to that of an elderly female patient during my intensive care unit rounds. I overheard this elderly female patient ask her nurse who I was. The nurse informed her that I was one of the attending physicians on the hospital medicine service, and she proceeded to tell her nurse that she had never seen a "woman doctor" before. With all the female colleagues I had at that time, I was baffled but happy to be her first introduction to women in medicine. Though I was amazed at this patient's reaction, I later found that notions regarding gender in medicine can be ingrained.

Another time I had an epiphany was when two gentlemen were working with me; one was a third-year medical student participating in his first internal medicine clerkship on my service and the other, a foreign medical graduate mentee who was shadowing to gain U.S. clinical experience for his residency application.

After an extensive lecture on our patient's pathology and progress, we walked into the room as part of our rounding routine. We were ready to discharge her home. After brief conversation, I performed a physical exam. While offering appropriate discharge directives for her condition I came to the point where I had to instruct her to follow up with her primary care doctor within one week from the time she left the hospital.

I said: "Ma'am, I would like you to go back to see Dr. Jones, and *he* will need to check —."

She quickly interrupted me with a look of disgust.

"You mean she; Dr. Jones is a woman."

Her facial expression gave away her disappointment in the fact that I did not know her doctor's gender. It was almost as if she assumed all the female doctors within a 10-mile radius would know and collaborate with one another.

"Maybe we should?" I thought to myself.

In that moment I felt ashamed. I too had become victim of an unconscious bias in my mind that her primary doctor was supposed to be male.

As humans we are susceptible to creating a conscious or subconscious bias. These are primarily based on our most common interactions and influences. Our influences are mostly determined by how and where we were raised, what we were taught in school or at the dinner table at home. Rarely, media or other social, religious, and political groups ingrain it in us. The sensitivity to racial bias is definitely higher than most others in part due to the course of history in America and the persistent societal injustices towards minorities. I am typically hesitant to attribute every unpleasant interaction between differing opinions in the workplace to racism or sexism alone, but that does not cancel out the occurrence of both issues in our supposedly forward culture today.

WHEN A PATIENT CAN FIRE A PHYSICIAN BASED ON HATE that's covered up as a racial, social, or religious preference, the essence of our roles in healing with medicine is diminished. I should admit that while this does not occur frequently, as a black female physician it is distressing when it does happen. Clinical competency, skill, and trustworthiness are important traits that doctors, both male and female, train equally hard and long to acquire. The invalidation of a physician's competence based on issues unrelated to work performance or legal or ethical mishaps should not be acceptable. A culture of love and appreciation should continuously be taught and emphasized in our schools, religious and social gatherings, and homes. We should choose to see people for who they truly are and not solely based on assumptions on gender or racial roles or historical patterns. A culture of tolerance would teach the future generations about the consciousness of stereotypes and guide them to create an alternative and modern mindset that accepts a difference from their relative "norm".

As healthcare providers we are not exempt from falling prey to a bias based on the medical practice culture or our upbringing. We should also remain cognizant of this during care delivery. As diversity in gender, race and religious background continues to thrive in medicine, repetitive showcasing of local medical talent and skill would be a great way to expose our communities to the power of open-mindedness and harness the strength of variety brewing around us.

24

THE EYES WHICH ASKED
TO LIVE

SURABHI BATRA, MD, AND VINOD K. BATRA, MD

"How much time?" the ICU attending asked me as I took my place in a small procedure suite, ready to tap a 5-year-old boy who was not sedated. "He is a difficult stick; it might be a while," the nurse interjected. I carefully examined the landmarks on his back, looked at them, and said, "Three minutes; we should be done soon." True to my word, shortly after the needle pierced his skin and then through the dura mater surrounding the spinal cord, clear drops of spinal fluid began to fill the test tube I held in my hand —in less than three minutes. My mind raced back into time.

It was my first year and perhaps my first week as an enthusiastic pediatric oncology fellow. It was exciting yet nerve-racking; my pager continuously beeping, calling back anxious parents, pediatricians and pharmacists, pretending to be the local expert in the field.

As I was getting ready to leave the hospital on a Friday evening after completing my daily tasks, my phone rang. The hospital operator connected me to the caller on the other end, and all I heard was someone wailing. I focused hard and tried to ask again, "Good evening! This is a hospital, and this is Dr. X, can you tell me the reason for your call?" Nothing but inconsolable cries that are still fresh in my mind ten years later. Confused about what to do, I was about to hang up when a man spoke, "This lady is in an urgent care, and they just told her that her child has cancer. Can you help her? I am just a bystander." I was numb. This was the first new diagnosis I was going to deal with as a fellow. After recovering my wits, I jotted down the name and number of the patient's location so I could talk to the physician and make arrangements for transfer.

As the patient was on his way to our hospital, I focused on arranging my thoughts, carefully planning and visualizing every step and action I would do as the patient was brought in: how I was going to deliver 'the news', which tests I would send, how I would talk to the family to help them get through this, and how I would cure this patient. In my brief visualization, I had already cured this patient and taken his treatment to completion. Suddenly my beautiful *coup de grace* was interrupted by the arrival of the transport team. My patient, Ethan had arrived with his mom, Amanda. As the stretcher rolled past me, our eyes met. A thin frail boy with beautiful curly hair and big brown eyes; the eyes of a dreamer; the face of an angel. In that face were eyes appearing scared and asking for help to ease all the pain with a thin faint smile that was trying to hide all those questions behind it. A tall beautiful lady walked behind him sobbing and holding his hand trying to assure him that all will be well.

After informing the attending, Dr. Miller, and putting on my white coat with my little notepad in my pocket, I followed them into the room. "Good evening! We spoke on phone a few hours ago; I am the oncology fellow..." Before I could complete my sentence, Amanda held my hand, "So it is not cancer right? He is too young; only old people get cancer."

Suddenly my well prepared 'new diagnosis talk' did not seem enough to answer her question. I was thankful for my attending who walked in just then and took over the discussion. I watched with admiration as she smoothly eased the flow of the discussion into a different direction. She made a few light-hearted remarks and asked a volunteer to play with the child while we went into a different room — THE room — with the mom.

"This could be an infection, right?" the mom exclaimed at the outset. My inclination would have been to dodge the question by saying the go-to doctor phrase 'until further testing'. However, that was not the approach my attending took.

She looked into the mother's eyes, held her hand, and said, "This is leukemia. I have looked at your child's peripheral blood smear," she repeated, as if the mom had not heard, "Your child has cancer."

No response, silence. She patiently waited and then passed on a box of Kleenex to the distraught and aghast woman on the other end of the table. Then they came, not one, not two, but many; tears flowed down her cheeks, her lips trembled, and sobs wracked her body. They embezzled her ability to speak or ask any further questions. Her world had been shattered.

The next few hours swept by in the lengthy discussion that ensued, detailing the treatment course, further testing, chemotherapy, and of course, the question which seems to be the most obvious but has the most complicated answer — how much time does he have? I blankly looked at my attending, hoping for her to say, "he has all the time; we will cure this!" She thought for a minute before explaining the complicated Kaplan-Meier curve for survival: how the numbers do not apply to an individual patient and how it was hard to predict where her son would sit on the curve. I took a few years to wrap my brain around this concept, but once I did, it made the most sense to me. Trying to be more precise than you can, did not confer any advantage to an oncologist, and to some extent it would have been irresponsible at the moment.

Interestingly, after a long hour or two of facts, numbers and emotion, what seemed like a haunting, malevolent, aggressive and ruthless adversary about an hour ago, childhood leukemia turned into an arduous phenomenon for which we seemed to have a solution. As we left the room together with the mother as a part of our team, we left ready to take on this challenge and cure her little angel.

The next day I performed my first procedure as an oncology fellow; our patient had a bone marrow and spinal tap. As it turned out, we could not sedate the patient, as would have been the normal protocol during the procedures, due to a huge mass growing between his chest and lungs posing ample sedation risks including respiratory failure and death. After carefully watching a YouTube video showing the technique of the procedures several times the night before, I thought I was well prepared.

As I entered the patient's room with a cheerful smile on my face, I explained the protocol and reviewed every detail, risks and benefits. Before I handed the consent form to the mother, she looked me in the eye and asked, "Doctor, how many of these have you done?" I was not expecting this question. Even though I had tried my hand at a few during residency and medical school, doing it on someone not sedated was unchartered territory for me. "None," I wanted to say, but caught myself.

I quickly said, "Well, I have done a few, but my attending has done innumerable, and she will be supervising me."

"Will it be painful?" Ethan asked. The mom gave me a questioning glance.

"Probably yes, but we will give you local anesthesia and some pain medicine prior to the procedure," I said.

The child, who was about seven years old, began to sob. As Amanda comforted him, our eyes met. Those eyes wanted a promise. A promise that her child would not be in pain. Those eyes begged me to save her child.

I arranged my armament: a spinal tap kit, drapes, needles, test tubes, bone marrow slides and chemotherapy which needed to be injected into the spinal fluid during the procedure. My attending took her place by my side, and I quickly revisited the steps of the procedure in my mind. We decided to do the spinal tap first. Cleaning, draping and local anesthesia, all went well. Then I picked up the needle, determined not to cause any pain. As my needle pierced through his skin, his back crunched in pain. I kept going, as would have been advised, and then could not go any further! Boom! Resistance! "Move the needle; you will be fine," my attending advised. I tried right, left, up and down trying to get into the space of his spine that holds the spinal fluid, but my needle would not move. Meanwhile, the little boy was writhing in pain, and his mom was in tears. I looked at them and withdrew my needle. My attending wanted me to try once more and assured me that every physician goes through these phases. My hands were shaking, but I was determined to get it right this time. As my patient hugged his mom tighter, and his cries increased in intensity, I tried my skills once again but to no avail. The patient's mother interjected and asked for me to leave the room and never see her child again.

Driving home later that evening, I fumbled through the radio stations, in an attempt to distract myself. As the band played the lyrics,"Without you I've got no hand to hold...," I felt tears streaming down my cheeks. Was it the self-made promise to keep the child pain free which I had not been able to keep, a feeling of failure or rejection, or the pain of giving that heart wrenching diagnosis to a mother and her child, or all of the above? I do not know. But I knew one thing, I was never going to see things the same again.

In the weeks and months that followed, I was not allowed to do his procedures or be a part of his care as per the request of the patient's mother. His clinic appointments were scheduled on days I was not present. I tried speaking to his mother a few times. I apologized to her for a bad experience at his first spinal tap. Dr. Miller even tried talking to her a few times, but it was in vain. I wanted to respect her wishes, but that did not stop me from being a part of his care. I would sincerely place all his orders prior to his appointment, make arrangements so that his procedures were as comfortable as possible, make sure he always had a child life specialist by his bedside and ample distraction during the procedures, and off and on take a peak at him while he was in clinic. He spent a few months in and out of the hospital due to ongoing complications, however as luck would have it, I was either away or on another service.

One fine afternoon, as I was rushing to my hematology clinic, a tiny hand grasped my finger. I turned around to see Ethan, now with no hair, big brown eyes, and a smile full of innocence looking into my eyes. "Why don't I see you anymore?" he asked. Before I could answer him, his mom came and took his hand away. They both turned around before disappearing down the hallway, she with anger, he with love and adoration.

ABOUT 6 MONTHS AFTER HIS INITIAL DIAGNOSIS, I WAS ON my hematology rotation when my phone rang. It was Dr. Miller, "Ethan has relapsed, and he is not a candidate for stem cell transplantation. We will be discussing him in today's meeting; I want you to be there." I was jarred. That afternoon the group concluded that Ethan would receive more intense chemotherapy; however, his prognosis remained dismal.

Weeks passed as I continued to work in the background with no upfront involvement. He had just completed his first round of very intense chemotherapy and was now awaiting recovery at home. It was an unusually busy weekend. I was on call and had not had a chance to go home yet; one after the other, my little patients kept me busy during the day. It was almost 9PM as I was heading towards the parking lot when my phone rang,

"Good evening, this is Dr..."

My sentence was cut off by a familiar voice, "Doctor, you remember Ethan, my little Ethan. His surgical scar, his abdomen, is opening up. It is red, and it's getting wider and wider." His mother's cries on the other end of the phone were heart wrenching.

This was not good. Was it the surgical scar sutures coming apart on his abdomen due to low blood counts caused by him receiving chemotherapy? Should I call the surgery team? Was it infection? As I rummaged my brain for answers, aloud I said, "Are you at home? I am going to send an air ambulance. It is necessary that he gets here as soon as possible, and I will be here to receive him so do not worry."

'Do not worry' – a phrase often used in my field and easier said than done. As I arranged his travel and informed Dr. Miller and the ICU, my phone rang again.

"They will not let me ride the ambulance, I will be driving. Will you stay by his side until I get there? Please Doctor, do not let him be scared."

I took a deep breath and absorbed what I heard. I was fighting tears. I was fighting fear; the fear of losing my first oncology patient. "Of course I will, you drive safely," I reassured her.

They airlifted him in less than 30 minutes. I spat out orders to the staff: IV fluids, antibiotics, intubation... whatever was needed to save him. Necrotizing fasciitis, a diagnosis of flesh eating bacteria in a patient with a low neutrophil count (infection fighting cells), leaving him immunocompromised was a very serious life threatening diagnosis. His mom was not here yet, but we needed to intubate him. With my knowledge of his condition, I knew he would not make it. Should we intubate him? Was it worth taking him through the ordeal? Should we wait for his mom so that she can hear his voice for one last time? As my mind played with these questions, I called her. "

How far are you? Will you be here soon?" I asked.

"It will take 30 minutes Doctor, there is traffic. Is everything ok? Will Ethan make it?" she asked.

"We are doing everything in our power, but we may need to intubate him. Is that ok?" I tried to sound as calm as possible.

"Of course it is fine; do whatever it takes and whatever you think is right. I trust your judgment."

And the phone disconnected as the weight of her words bore down on me, I realized the responsibility I had just been handed. What was the right decision? What was my judgment?

We did go ahead with the intubation and treatment until his mom, his sole guardian in the world, got there. I held his little hand in mine and hugged him for one last time, reassuring him that it was going to be ok as he was sedated and those beautiful brown eyes saw the light for the last time. By the time his mother got there, he was sedated, intubated and transcended into oblivion. What followed was a blur. With our help Amanda made a conscious choice not to resuscitate him and make his journey as comfortable as possible. Life support was removed the following day, and he rested in his own sweet world where there was no suffering, no more pain...

Days passed; weeks passed, and years passed. I often wonder what would Amanda be doing. I want to pick up the phone and call her. But what would I say? I want to say, "I'm sorry," as I could not save her child, but is it appropriate? Would that help? I do not know the answer to those questions, but Ethan's short life left an imprint on me. His big brown eyes often remind me of my reasons for choosing this profession, its sacredness, and why we need to keep moving forward.

✷ 25 ✷

THAT THURSDAY IN SEPTEMBER

ANGELA FREEHILL BROWN, MD

I found the lump on a Thursday night in the shower. A nighttime shower was unusual for me because the twins typically fight sleep, and I almost never get time to myself until late at night. But, it had been a hot Indian summer day and a long day in the clinic seeing patients. The twins fell asleep early; I needed that shower. I had been having pain in my left breast for about two weeks, and I had been mashing and smashing the tissue there, trying to find something, to no avail. But, when I raised my arm in the shower to wash my hair that night, I pushed at the top of the breast, near that tender spot, and there it was — a pea sized lump.

It hurt when I pressed, and to be sure, I pressed hard again. Yes, it was definitely there. I took a deep breath. Suddenly, I went cold, in spite of the hot water beating down on me. I switched off the water, not even sure if I had finished washing my hair. I felt fear overtake me, and I needed to sit down...and think. I wracked my brain and tried to think back to my medical school teaching on painful breast masses. I was an orthopedic surgeon so painful breast lumps were not in my everyday wheelhouse. I tried to be clinical, objective. My beating heart pounded in my ears, and I felt anything but clinical.

'This is a case of a 47 year old white female, healthy, overweight, type A, poor diet, 3 years out from In Vitro and a twin pregnancy.' I mentally checked off the boxes. The cancer word was circling my brain like a neon sign signaling 'Danger! Danger!' I thought about the things that were in my favor. I had breastfed my three children. I had no family history of breast cancer. I was young, well, I guess, young-ish...not super young in years but physiologically young...and so strong. Even though I had a bit of extra weight, I had always prided myself on being strong. I would go out of my way to choose the hard things. I decided early on as a kid that I wanted to have a life with lots of amazing things: vacations, homes, and incredible experiences. I learned soon after college graduation that my degree in psychology wasn't going to provide this life so I set my sights on medical school. Orthopedic surgery was my answer for how I was going to make this life for myself. I loved being a surgeon. I loved the gratification of helping others get better and restoring function. I loved the idea of fixing things. I most definitely was the Fixer in the family.

I got dressed after completing my mental assessment. My heart was still pounding but slowing a little now. I walked into the living room where my husband was watching some mindless TV show. I sat on the couch silently, and he didn't really even look up. I sat staring at the television, not seeing or watching, just looking straight ahead. I thought this moment was probably going to change the course of our lives. I had a bad feeling. I was pretty sure, after all, that this painful lump was not going to be a good thing. I was pretty sure I had just found breast cancer, and I was terrified. My twin girls were just three, and my ten year old daughter was just starting to enter the beginning stages of puberty. My husband and I, as a couple, had just gotten over the trauma of five years of miscarriages, infertility, a failed IVF and then a successful IVF followed by a very difficult twin pregnancy. There had been so much emotional upheaval with all of that. My orthopedic practice was just now recovered after the personal time away dealing with my health. We were finally coming out of the tunnel of lost wages and lost time. The kids were finally in a routine, sleeping better, and manageable. We had talked just the other day about how we were feeling like we were able to relax a little bit, that we were entering such a great time in our lives. We were keenly aware how lucky we were to have healthy kids, a beautiful home, no worries except where to go for holidays. It was all about to change, again. I hated to even say it out loud.

I gulped and swallowed and gripped the edge of the sofa. I sat forward, tense, and I took a deep breath.

"Honey, hey -could you turn that tv down for a sec?"

He looked up, surprised. I could see him looking at me, leaning forward. I could see the concern on his face at my tone. I pressed on.

"Okay, so I don't really know how to say this so I will just blurt it out. I was just in the shower, and I found a lump in my breast...and I am kind of worried."

"What?" he said. His voice was shrill in my ears. "You found a lump? In your breast?" he repeated my words. I felt nauseous. I nodded, but I didn't know what else to say. He just looked at me, needing more. I nodded again and cleared my throat.

"Yes, I did. I need to call in the morning and schedule a mammogram, but I have been having a weird pain in the top of my left breast for a couple weeks. I thought I might have pulled a muscle lifting the girls or dragging luggage through the airport when we came back from the beach last month, but I found this lump tonight, and now I think it is something more."

It was his turn to process. He set the remote down on the side table and looked at me. He was not a medical guy, but he was smart. He could hear the unspoken 'cancer' word loud and clear, and it was evident from his face; he was worried too.

I spoke again, "I just need to call and get scheduled for the mammogram. We won't know anything until we get that done. But, I just had to tell you what was going on."

He nodded his understanding. "But, you are going to be ok, right? I mean, you are young and healthy so this probably isn't..." His voice trailed off.

"Breast cancer...", I finished for him. "I don't know. It might be. I pray no, but why else would I have a lump?"

There it was. We had spoken it out loud, and now the cancer card was on the table. Just like that, a normal Thursday night in September had turned into a night we would never forget. The cancer train had entered the station, and we had just boarded.

That night as we went to bed, he held my hand, and I felt comforted. Yet, in just moments, he was asleep, and I was left alone with my racing thoughts. In the darkness, I gingerly moved my fingers over the top of my breast. Again and again, I examined that firm blob of tissue. My mind reeled, and I tried to slow down my thoughts and my breath. Fear pulsed through me as I shivered in the darkness. This cannot be real. The stillness of the lonely night answered me with the harsh reality that it was. Somehow, some way, I finally slept, dreading the day to come.

The next morning, I promised my husband I would call him the minute I knew anything. I dropped the girls off and drove to the clinic, mentally preparing myself for the phone call. I got to the parking lot five minutes early, and I called my own hospital and spoke to the operator, "Hi, this is Dr. Freehill, I need mammography please."

I waited on hold less than a minute then a cheerful young woman answered the phone. "This is the Breast Health Center, how may I help you?"

I inwardly cringed. I was calling about an issue that I was pretty sure wasn't about "health". I answered back, "Yes, hello. This is Dr. Freehill; I am calling about a personal matter, and I would like to schedule a mammogram please." She asked my birthday, and I could hear her fingers clicking the computer keys in the background.

She piped back up, "Yes, I see here that you had one last December so we can schedule you for December of this year. Your insurance will only pay for one mammogram a year, Ma'am."

"Um, no. That is not going to work. I have a concerning lump that I found, and I can't wait that long. I need to come in today."

She paused, and my heart nearly bounded out of my chest. "We do not have spots today, Doctor, and to get a quicker appointment, I would recommend you call your primary care physician to get the order. We would need to do a focused mammogram with possible ultrasound-guided biopsy the same day, and we need an order for that."

I hung up. I had a sudden realization of helplessness. I was not in charge here. I was suddenly a patient on the receiving end of the healthcare system and bureaucracy. I was at the mercy of the schedulers, the receptionists, and the secretaries. I was not able to direct all of this to my liking unlike my every day gig. I had to follow the rules and make the calls and do what everyone else had to do to get my scan; I didn't like it.

I dialed my primary physician's office, and when the receptionist picked up, I asked for her nurse. Even though I was late for my own office hours, I had to get this taken care of.

"Tammy, this is Angela Freehill. I am calling about a personal matter. I found a breast lump last night, and I need an order for a mammogram with a possible ultrasound guided biopsy sent over to the hospital please. I am very worried it might be breast cancer, and I need it ASAP. Can you do that for me, please?"

My voice broke as I squealed out my last word, and I felt the tears rushing to my eyes for the first time. Why me? Why now? How could this happen? Questions and fury were swirling inside me, and I knew I just needed to calm down.

She was so kind, "Oh sweetie, I am so sorry. Let me call over there. I will send the order right now, and let me see what I can do for you. I will call you back, OK?"

I was able to murmur OK as I hung up. When I walked into clinic, I smiled at my nurses and started my day. Just like that — I turned it off — tuned it out. I felt like I might vomit, but I was not about to let anyone know. I was strong, remember?

Later that afternoon, I got the call. My mammogram was scheduled for Wednesday morning at 8am. It was the Friday of Labor Day weekend, and Wednesday was the absolute earliest they could get me in. I had no idea how I was going to wait that long.

That night, my kids jumped on my lap, and my husband made a meal. We swam an end-of-summer late night swim, and we watched a movie. Nothing was different at all, and yet everything was changed for me. The smallest moments made me catch my breath. One of the twins fell asleep in my arms, and as I tenderly carried her up the stairs and laid her in bed, I whispered a plea to heaven, "Please God, let me live. Please, oh please, let me be ok. I cannot leave them."

Several times over the weekend, my husband and I locked

eyes, and each time he hugged me extra tight; each time tears sprang quickly to my eyes. The days passed in an anxious blur; I kept hoping it was just a bad dream.

Finally, after what seemed like a year, Wednesday morning arrived. Wednesday was my usual day in the OR so I had bumped my cases back to 10:30 am. I was late for my appointment. I was always late for things, mostly because I wanted to spend the time with the kids in the mornings, but they were an extra challenge that day. I rushed into the mammogram center frantic and breathing hard. As I wrote my name on the sheet and looked around, I realized I had never been inside this space even though I walked by it every day. It was a pleasant yet bland area with the television blaring an advertisement jingle. I waited.

The technician fetched me, and she dropped me in the room. After I wrapped the pink papery gown around my shoulders open in the front, she ushered me into the mammography suite where it was dark and hushed inside. She was efficient and confident while at the same time gentle and kind. As she kept repositioning my left breast in different angles against the cold machine, I had a vision of this horrible spiculated mass with long fingers reaching across the expanse of my breast. Finally, we finished, and she asked if I wanted to see the images. I did. When I turned my eyes to the screen, I could see it from across the room: a mass shaped like a small grape sat right at the top of my breast. "That's it?" I thought to myself, "Well, that doesn't look so bad." It was little, maybe one centimeter, oval with no irregular edges, no spiculations, no long reaching fingers. She said, "The radiologist will be right in," as she scurried out of the room.

The radiologist that day was a colleague of mine. I often called him to review MRI's I was unsure of. I trusted and liked him. His boy even went to school with my oldest. After he walked in and said hello, we got down to business.

"Angela, this looks like a cyst to me. It is round and has no irregularity. I think we can just watch this and maybe have you come back in a month for a follow-up scan."

My heart dropped. I thought about just running out of there, carrying on with my life as if this lump was not even there. But then I felt the familiar stab of pain I had been having over the last month, and my words tumbled out, "No way."

He was clearly taken aback. I was assertive, and cut right to the point. "I have been having pain here for a month, and I just found this lump last week. I will not be able to rest until I know this is not breast cancer. We are getting a biopsy today...now. I mean, please..."

I looked up at him. My jaw was set, and I could feel my teeth clench together. He said, "Don't you have surgery today? Why don't we do this another day? You could come back next week? You will be sore today if we do this now."

"It's ok if I am sore. I truly just want to get this over with. I am staying until we get this done. I will deal with the rest of my day later." I had stood my ground, and he looked at me quizzically, just for a second, then he nodded, "Ok then. Let's go."

He guided me to the ultrasound room, and the tech there smiled at me. I knew her too, from my child's school. I felt like the whole town was going to know the intricacies of my breast issue before long. I signed the papers, and we made small talk about the weekend and the weather while I impatiently waited for some insurance guy on the other end of the phone to give his approval.

Finally, we were underway. As the radiologist went over the lump with the ultrasound wand, I squinted hard, trying to determine if there was blood flow. I didn't think one time about modesty or embarrassment. My eyes were laser focused on the screen. I saw the dark shadow of the lump, but I couldn't see much else.

"OK," he said. "I am going to aspirate this with a needle to see if I can get any fluid out. If we don't get fluid out, we will take a sample of the tissue and send it off."

He numbed me up and plunged the needle into the top of my breast. I watched to see the needle pass right into the mass on the screen, and then, nothing. There was no fluid. It was clearly solid. He cleared his throat.

"Ok, then, this was not fluid- filled, like I thought. I am going to take some tissue samples now."

I was numb: physically and emotionally. I just wanted it over with. I wanted to run away. We finished, and once the radiologist left the room, I sprinted upstairs, clutching an ice pack to my chest.

My surgery day was difficult. I was distracted and the cases were not easy. I made it through, but it was not my best work that day. I felt human and fallible all day: vulnerable and exposed.

The next morning, I dropped off the kids and then walked into my office. I started my day with my scheduled patients, but every time my beeper or my phone went off, I jumped. I knew that my fate was laying on a pathologist's desk, and I was itching to know, to face it. By 9:30 that morning, I could not take it any longer. I slipped out of the clinic area, wandered down the hall to my office, and closed the door. I picked up the phone and dialed the hospital.

"Pathology, please," I inquired when the hospital operator answered. She clicked me over, and I believed I could feel the hum of the phone line in my veins. The pathologist answered gruffly, "Hello."

I stammered, "Um, yes, hello. This is Angela Freehill. I am calling on a personal matter. I had a breast biopsy yesterday; I am pretty sure my slides are on your desk, and I would just love to know the results, please."

He answered back quickly, "Yes, I have your slides right here. I have read them." He continued on, "This is highly unusual though. We usually have the nurse call patients with the results. This is not my job."

I did my best to control my irritation. I tried not to sound hysterical. "Well, yes, I know it is not your job. I am calling to ask for a personal favor so I do not have to wait all day for this. If you could just tell me...please," I finished.

The world stood still. The pause was thick with his tension and my fear. I was dizzy with anxiety. He spoke quickly then and without emotion. "Invasive ductal carcinoma, high grade. Tumor markers have been sent, and they will take a week to come back." I sucked in my breath, and I looked at the clock. 9:37 am.

I muttered, "Ok then, thank you so much, I will talk to you later then."

The first thing I thought as I hung up the phone was how stupid I sounded, telling him I would talk to him later. The second thing I thought was that I was now a woman with breast cancer. Yesterday, I had hope. This morning at 8:34 and at 9:12 and at 9:33, I still had hope. Now, I was a woman with breast cancer, and it was the loneliest and most hopeless feeling in the world. I dialed my husband, and all of a sudden, I was sobbing into the phone. He told me to breathe. I realized I had a clinic full of patients and a roomful of nurses and receptionists just going on with their normal days waiting for their doctor. I told my husband to just wait and that I was coming home.

I stood up and felt the warm tears falling down my cheeks. I realized I had never understood the warrior analogies I had heard before of women dealing with cancer. But I felt like I understood all in one epic moment. I wanted to live. I wanted to fight and do whatever it took to see my children grow and to hold my husband's hand night after night. I felt like I was ready to go to battle and to do whatever it took to slay the monster. I was afraid, but I would not run. As I got out of my chair and walked down the hall, the hot tears were still coming. I squared my shoulders and decided, yes, I was going to fight. I wanted to live, and I would fight as long as I had a breath. I wanted to LIVE.

LOVE AT FIRST SIGHT

YULIA JOHNSON, DO

A t the age of 12 and as the only child, my age of innocence ended as I became the primary caregiver of my mother in a the country with the most horrific health care you can imagine. I was living in Ukraine in 1984 when my mom was diagnosed with the fatal, self-destructing disease of the liver called primary biliary cirrhosis (in simple terms it means your own immune system attacks your liver and destroys it). The only cure is a liver transplant, and in my country in 1984, and even today, it was and still is equivalent to the medicine from another planet.

Every citizen was entitled to free universal health care in the former Soviet Union, yet to see a doctor or be hospitalized you had to pay a bribe to everyone from doctors to nurses for every minute of their time, every shot, even every administered medication. The first time visiting my mom in the hospital ward horrified me as I saw moldy walls, filthy sheets, and screaming nurses. Patients lined hospital corridors moaning without any attention from the nurses; some even sat or laid on the floors. Those that had a bed, had to bring sheets from home or they laid on the metal springs with no mattress. The restroom floors were soaking wet and muddy, and the toilets were jammed full of urine and feces. The only sink was full of blood; there was no running water between the hours of 9am and 6pm.

I held back tears and was filled with anger and despair! It was so unfair that I would lose my mom so young. How would I go on without her? I was the only child, and she was my best friend. We eventually sold everything out of our 200 square foot apartment to keep up the basic IV multivitamins, IV fluids, and doctor's appointments. We begged and bribed the doctors to look at her once every few days in the hospital; we bribed nurses with American dollars for every injection and basic aspirin. By the time I was 16 years old, I was a pro at getting her vitamins and IV fluids on the black market. Dark alleys of the city became all too familiar to me. Getting her next week's supply of basic vitamin injections and medications, IV supplies and IV bags sounds like a scene from a Godfather movie to you, but it was the reality I lived. Leaving the country was not an option back then for us; no one was permitted to leave Soviet Union. The last straw before we started our journey of immigration as refugees was my mother breaking her hip from a fall on the bus.

She needed a surgery to secure her hip bones in place, or she would never be able to walk. In order to do that, a four inch metal rod would have to be secured through the hip bone. (Even now I get sick to my stomach recalling the events of that week and the surgery day itself.) We had enough money for the surgeon and everything they needed in the operating room, but at the last minute there was not enough for the anesthesia according to the people helping to organize it all. I could not have imagined what would transpire next. As though nothing happened, they started the surgery and operated on my mother with no anesthetic. The operating room was not too far from where we were told to wait, and my father and I both heard my mother's blood curdling screaming for what felt like an eternity and then silence. The numbness filled my heart and my body as I imagined in that moment that my mom was gone. As we later learned, she passed out from the intensity of the pain, and they used that as her anesthesia for the remainder of the procedure.

Over the course of my mother's illness, I grew more and more resentful of medicine and everything it represented in my country. Every time my mom was hospitalized, I began to realize that I really enjoyed taking care of people and not just her. I started helping other patients with their needs in the hospital as well as helping their families navigate the Soviet health care system.

🐦

FAST-FORWARD TO A HOT SUMMER DAY OF AUGUST IN 1992. I still remember stepping onto Ellis Island and looking up at the Statue of Liberty in complete awe, full of excitement and hope. The hot and salty air of New York City greeted us with what I could only describe today as a smell of freedom. From delicate to overpowering, an enticing mix of fresh hot dogs, warm crepes, tacos, Indian curry, pretzels, beer and car exhausts all liberated by the heat of that summer day. It was the happiest day of my life, and the day that would change our lives forever. After five years of legal paperwork, we finally were able to leave; my family immigrated as Jewish refugees to the United States. Our final destination was Denver, Colorado.

I was married then and pregnant with twins, and my mother was in a wheelchair after only a few months since her hip surgery. I cannot put together words to describe the full gamut of emotions that day that were flying through me. One minute I felt paralyzed with fear, "How will we survive without a word of English?" followed by complete and overwhelming joy to be free, accepted and welcomed to a new amazing country with medical care for my mom.

After my experiences in Ukraine, to describe my first encounter with modern medicine in the US would be like trying to describe someone's first flight to the moon in a space shuttle. By the time we came to the US, Mom's condition was declining fast; she was emaciated, and she could hardly speak or recognize faces. She was almost immediately hospitalized at the University of Colorado hospital. For days we could barely contain the tears; we were so overwhelmed by the kindness of everyone caring for her. The stress of caring for my mom along with the tremendously hard and long move across the continents took a toll on my body, and no matter how hard I tried to be careful and rest, I went into premature labor, and my twin boys were born ten weeks premature.

The neonatal intensive care nursery became our home for the two months following their birth. They would not have survived in Ukraine; there were no NICU's with incubators there and no way of keeping preemies alive. Knowing this I just could not contain my gratitude to the medical profession in my new home in the US. I was hooked. I was addicted to medicine here. It was a love at first sight. I knew I wanted to be a part of it. I just wasn't sure how a 20 year old girl, now a newly divorced single mom who spoke no English, would accomplish it. I knew that I wanted to be there for people. I wanted to be a part of the culture that makes so much of a difference in people's lives. I began my course work while continuing to take care of my mom and my twin boys: always balancing my courses and my responsibilities of being the caregiver for my mother and children. I became an EMT and worked night shifts on the ambulance which left my days wide open for school work, my mom's care and of course my twin boys. I loved my job as an EMT. I felt it was my first real responsibility for someone's life.

I will never forget my first patient asking if I was sure she needed to go to the hospital. She looked to me with profound trust believing that I had all the knowledge and experience to help her make the right decision. The feeling was heavy with responsibility and came with recognition of my role in this person's life. No one can teach you about that feeling, and no one prepares you for what it will mean to you. It is born right there, in those fleeting moments of you having to make life and death decisions, in those looks and unspoken words. It is that feeling that kept driving my sleepless nights and long college courses, and it is that feeling that I could not have imagined giving up.

A few years later, as my mom's disease progressed further, she was placed on a waiting list for a liver transplant. Five minutes after my last biology exam of my junior year, the transplant pager went off, just a few days before my mother's 58th birthday. I spent my spring break in the hospital with her and could not have imagined a better gift. She came home after a successful operation the following Sunday, and with the help of my family and friends I was able to finish the spring semester and continue to care for my mom.

As you can imagine learning English, being a single mom, working full time, and being my mom's sole caregiver were not for the faint of heart. But my love for this country and its people were constant reminders and inspiration to keep going. Nothing was ever going to stop me from becoming a doctor.

MY ACCEPTANCE LETTER TO MEDICAL SCHOOL CAME JUST two weeks after my mom passed away. We had come home with her in hospice two weeks prior. One of the last meaningful conversations we had was about my future and my journey for the last eight years in this country. It was one of the best talks I shared with my mom — one of the things I miss the most since she has been gone. I took the MCAT four times to get a good enough score to apply for medical school. My English was still not fast enough to nail the verbal reasoning portion of the test, but after two years of trying I finally did it.

A few short months later I was sitting in the auditorium filled with many aspiring young student doctors while fighting tears of joy to be there and sorrow that she could not share this day with me. Four years of medical school flew by faster than I could have imagined. My days were filled with my now eight year-old twin boys, hundreds of pages of new information to learn everyday, lectures, simulated patient assessment labs, and much more. Every new day felt like drinking out of the fire hose, yet I could not get enough of it. I loved all of my rotations and quickly realized that I would become a primary care doctor.

I am not going to lie; some mornings I woke up and wondered if I was doing the right thing, or if I was crazy to do this with two kids. But at the end of the day, it was always worth it. My children were my biggest inspiration in medical school and my biggest motivators to do my best. Today they are 25 years old, and one of them is a medical student as well following in my footsteps. His brother is in law school, and I could not be more proud of the amazing young men they have become.

Growing up in Ukraine and being my mother's caregiver since I was a young girl was hard, devastating, and gruesome. I have wished so many times that my mom was healthy, and I was able to be a kid again. But, if my wish came true, I would have never realized my desire to care for people and to become a physician. I would not have learned what it feels like to give hope, love, compassion, and a gift of your soul to others, and what it is like to be on the receiving end. For that I am eternally grateful. Our life experiences, no matter how hard and impossible they may seem, shape us and our future. They shape how we see the world and what we give to the world. Lean in to them, embrace them, and you may be surprised what may become your love at first sight.

❧ 27 ❧

LEDGE

MARIA PEREZ-JOHNSON, DO, FAAP

Elisa could count the failures thankfully on one hand. But oh my God, that hand was almost full. She, like most, came into this profession to help people, to make them better, to find cures, to first do no harm, but when mistakes are made or errors occur, it cuts her to her soul. She is left with nothing but a large hole right where her passion, drive, and confidence stem. How can she reconcile her errors with her passion to heal? How does she continue to work without confidence in her capability?

The drive to become a physician had always been with Elisa. Her family would state that she told everyone she met that she wanted to be a doctor ever since she was a little girl; after all, she had been putting Band-Aids on her teddy bear since she was a toddler. Perhaps that life quest was true, or perhaps it was just her parents' dream and their way to encourage her in her endeavor. Everyone knew she was capable, she was extremely intelligent and strong willed, but no one would ever realize the cost. What is the price of an education, the price of dinners away from family, the emotional cost of holidays, nights, and weekends spent apart? What is the price of the emotional toil, of the stress, grief, shock, and death encountered on every shift, in every week, in every month, and in every year. What is the value of self-doubt; what worth is her life? What to do? How much more should she lean in or lean out? How long until she lets go? Just one more step over the edge...

It's now May, and it's graduation season. High school, college, and today medical school. How many years to get to this point, too many years to count, and it's not even the end of her training. In reality it's just the beginning. Elisa walks just past the library where several classmates are already gathered. The ceremony is about to commence, and trivial paperwork was required prior to the start. It will probably be the last time she will step foot into this building; the building that has consumed so many of her hours over the last four years. She looks up and sees her corner window. Many, many, many days she had spent there, well over twelve hours at a time, and honestly much closer to fifteen to eighteen hours crammed into that corner cubicle.

The library was six floors; each floor held numerous books and a wealth of knowledge. Each floor was designed with cubicles at the periphery that allowed students to study with a window and a view of the city: views of surrounding neighborhoods and depending on the side of the building, panoramic views of downtown skyscrapers. Views that were spectacular during the day and even more vivid at night. The library had sixteen to twenty-four rooms that were highly coveted each day, and given to the student that arrived early enough and thus would be allowed to camp out in that cubicle for the day. It would give a view to the outside world, a world away from textbooks, quizzes, and exams. The library had access to reference books, study materials, models, and video and audio of lectures as well as additional study aids that were necessary to tackle the tremendous amount of material that she needed to master. It became her second home for the first two academic years of medical school.

Done with the trivial paperwork, she heads back out of the library onto the sidewalk and out onto the parking lot. Her van is full of parents, brother, husband, and kids. No one would ever have thought that she would have been able to make it to this point carrying this load of material and these many souls along for the ride. It was a roundabout way to get here, and by all means she would be considered a role model, an inspiration to others. As she maneuvers the parking lot, it is only a short distance across the street to the auditorium where the commencement ceremony will be taking place.

She enters another parking lot and finds a suitable location close enough to the entrance that the kids and her elderly parents can maneuver without much effort. She is about an hour early but wanted to ensure that parking and seating would not be an issue for her family. As she enters the large auditorium, she secures a comfortable location for her family to view the ceremony and discusses a meeting spot to rendezvous following the event. Elisa then proceeds to the back of the stage to dress in her cap and gown. She will be hooded by a family friend who is a PhD and made the trip to be at her side for this special occasion. The professor has been her inspiration and one of her greatest champions.

She has already learned a lot, the amount of knowledge gained is exponential, and she is just at the start of her career. She is a mom, and therefore she chose her upcoming specialty in order to ease the pain of long hours and time spent away from her family. Not that she hasn't loved her chosen specialty, but had she not had a husband and kids, her choice may have been different. She spent the first two years of medical school away from her kids and husband. Her husband was serving in the US Navy and stationed aboard a navy carrier in the South Pacific, and her children were with her parents to ease the burden of medical school and to give them a more stable home front. She was not the only medical student with kids; a few of her classmates even had babies while in school, but as she was essentially a single mother since her husband was deployed, it was more reasonable to have her kids stay with her parents during the first few years of school. Given that fact, she drove home every other weekend – a six hour drive each way. The time spent away was hard; she cried the moment she left the kids and continued to cry until she reached Waco, Texas. By the time she reached Fort Worth, she had regained her composure and was ready to tackle the week.

Her classmates knew better than to ask her how the kids were for fear that an onslaught of tears would ensue, and she battled back the tears of separation daily. Once back at school, the routine and coursework would take up her time, the weeks would pass, and she would then be back at home after another round of exams. She was a good student, passing classes easily, and she passed her board exams with no difficulty. At the top of her class, she had a great foundation on which to begin her internship and residency.

She chose pediatrics and was excited about the possibility of truly making a difference in the lives of the families she would encounter. Grueling hours awaited as this was a time long before the residency boards approved changes in hourly limits for interns and residents. Often times she spent 36 hours or more awake in the NICU or on the floors usually without more than a few minutes to an hour of sleep at best. Post call, after a 36 hour shift, she often picked up the kids from school and took them to an early matinee. This served two purposes: the obvious one of entertainment with a cheap meal, as well as the not so obvious one in that it allowed her the ability to sleep some before she made the hour drive home. Sleep deprivation was something that was not just expected; it was bragged upon. It was also old school and looked on as a rite of passage. Three years later residency was complete, and she easily passed her boards and became an official board certified pediatrician. She began work in a clinic then after some time, she moved on to work in a pediatric emergency room where the cases were more dramatic. While she missed the connection of being a family pediatrician, the enticement of emergency medicine kept her on her toes, and she was both fulfilled and excited about her work. So much so that often looking back at her most recent cases she could list the several traumatic and life changing experiences.

PATIENT 1: On one random weeknight close to the end of her shift, around 5am, after the emergency room had been cleared out and everybody was winding down, a twenty year old female walked into the pediatric emergency room carrying something in a towel. Elisa was called to this patient's room for a spontaneous delivery, and found a baby en caul delivery at 24 weeks. This type of delivery occurs 1:80,000. It's a delivery where the baby is still encased in the amniotic sac. She ruptured the sac, started CPR, and successfully intubated this small preterm infant who weighed only 500 grams. The baby did well and eventually graduated from the NICU to later go home without any long term complications. There was a LIFE saved that day, amazing work, and she was thankful she was able to get that endotracheal tube in. GOD is good.

PATIENT 2: Another case on a Sunday afternoon, with typical ER traffic all day until the HALO helicopter called with a heads up on a set of siblings that were involved in a major motor vehicle accident. There were some minor injuries per report. The patients arrived via HALO to our trauma bays. All the essential work-up ordered, and all the patients appeared stable and without significant findings. The 18 month old male began calling Elisa "momma" from the bed as she held his hand while labs were being drawn. She later learned his mother, who was driving, and his grandfather who was also a passenger in the vehicle both perished in the accident. LIVES SAVED and LIVES LOST, Elisa was heartbroken for the family. She left the room with tears streaming down her face in the hallway, and later returned to the room and hugged the baby until his relatives arrived.

PATIENT 3: On a Monday afternoon, just around 3pm, another impeding motor vehicle crash was announced. An 18 month old restrained passenger was brought in via EMS (emergency medical service). The father was a firefighter and thus the hallway was full of fellow paramedics, and additional firemen. The patient was stable. He was an active, alert and rambunctious 18 month old with whom the staff quickly fell in love with. He was without evidence of injury. Unfortunately, the mother of the patient was dead on the scene (DOS). Even now Elisa can still hear the wails of the father when he found out his wife had died. They had just closed on a mortgage loan for a new home that morning. A child's LIFE was saved; yet, life can be so unfair.

PATIENT 4: On a weekday, just before lunch an unknown age female, Jane Doe, was brought in non-responsive by her friend. She was exhibiting agonal respirations as she gasped for air. She was of thin frame, and looked like a drug user. Elisa gave her a life saving medication called Narcan to reverse the effects of a suspected opioid overdose. Following the Narcan administration, the patient developed spontaneous respirations, but then became combative. The patient was angry and began to spit blood on everyone, but while staff attempted to restrain her, she became apneic again. She was then intubated in order to protect her airway to assess where the blood was coming from while labs were obtained and more extensive exams were done. Once she was stable, she was transferred to an adult facility for more definitive care. Her family later confirmed that she was a long time drug user with previous overdoses. Her LIFE was saved that day due to a medication that reverses opioids – Elisa felt both sympathy and frustration for the family personally dealing with the effects of the opioid epidemic.

PATIENT 5: On a weeknight, CPS (child protective services) called ahead to inform the ER of an infant being brought in for suspected abuse. This was an infant, who had previously been seen for non-accidental trauma and suspected abuse, and was now brought in for suspicion of abuse again. On exam, the patient had an enlarged head with multiple bruises with the head CT scan was positive for new skull fractures. The infant then became apneic with difficulty maintaining arousal and respirations. Elisa intubated and admitted the patient to the pediatric intensive care unit. LIFE SUCKS – PEOPLE SUCK. After caring for this patient, she rushed to the bathroom and cried. The patient was pronounced brain dead the next day.

PATIENT 6: On an uneventful Saturday afternoon around 4pm, a 40 year old thin male walked into the Pediatric ER with chest pain after playing basketball with his son. He had a significant ST segment elevation on his EKG that looked similar to the shape of a fireman's hat indicating a possible heart attack (the more technical term: acute myocardial infarction). Elisa started standard STEMI (ST elevation, acute MI) protocols: labs, morphine, oxygen, nitroglycerin, aspirin, etc. The patient was reported to have elevated troponin enzymes on his lab report which was also concerning for acute MI signifying that there was heart damage. Phone calls to the EMS, cardiology, catheterization laboratory were all ensued. Thankfully for the patient, from the time he came into the emergency room door and was rushed to catheterization lab took only 45 minutes—well below that national standard. The patient's heart had a 95% blockage of his LAD, left anterior descending artery (the widow maker) — Elisa saved a LIFE that day; it was a good day...as a pediatrician dealing with an acute myocardial infarction was something Elisa learned in medical school and in training, but she didn't take care of these on a daily basis. She was scared but was able to save this adult's life that day.

⚜

WHAT ELISA HASN'T LISTED AND WHAT WEIGHS MORE heavily on her heart and soul are the losses. Yes, some of the above are lives lost, but many of those were expected. The ones that sting and become too much to bear are the ones in which a questionable outcome or unexpected turn of events caused an unforeseen death.

The cases that are harder are the ones where she worked for hours to revive someone and her efforts were still not enough or the tragedies where an unforeseen event such as a simple "he slipped out the back door and fell into the pool" caused such immense pain and sudden death. These recurrent events and loss of lives weighed heavily on her soul. Unfortunately following a tragedy there is no rest, she has to move onto the next patient; the waiting rooms were always full and the doors always open. The what ifs, or what could've been or should've been always come to mind. She never thought medicine would be so hard.

Often times there are no resources for wounded physicians, like Elisa, to find outreach to reconcile these events. The slew of committees and peer reviews can feel more punitive, and thus physicians like her are often left to fend for themselves. Constant self-doubt can be an overwhelming burden; the fear of losing their license or livelihood keeps many from seeking help. Often they turn to drugs or alcohol. Balancing the good outcomes should balance the poor ones; yet, unfortunately it doesn't work that way. Two good for one bad is not the same; thousands of good outcomes for one bad outcome is not equivalent. Each poor outcome, missed diagnosis, or bad procedure cast an even larger shadow of doubt than the numerous saves that a physician may have made. How to reconcile these events is something that the medical profession is just starting to ponder. However, Elisa already has made her decision. Elisa takes a deep breath and steps off the edge...

The cases listed above are true experiences. The contemplation of suicide and the actual suicide are inspired by a real event where a physician stepped off the edge of her apartment building. The consequences of physician suicide are so great and disheartening that I, the author of this chapter, felt a need to address both the great and tragic side of this profession.

Each physician gives countless hours away to develop their skills and training. The average medical student leaves school with close to $250,000 in debt. The countless hours spent studying and in training make each physician a valuable commodity; yet now more than ever the medical profession is being attacked, and physician suicide rates are at an all-time high. Anywhere from 300-400 physicians commit suicide yearly — the equivalency to almost one suicide a day (29.1/month)[10].

More resources are needed to aid physicians in dealing with the onslaught emotion that occurs with a bad outcome. Yes, perhaps more training or education may be required, but more often than not, the errors are just that. Physicians are not gods — they are not infallible — they are people who make mistakes — human. Peer review and medical staff committees need to assist those that they govern without punitive actions. We need physicians; we need good, quality, caring physicians.

❧ 28 ❧

SELF-CARE IS BETTER PATIENT CARE

NINA LUM, MD

"Self Care Is Better Patient Care."
- Unknown

It was a warm evening in mid-July when the unexpected happened. July is the most threatening month for teaching hospitals because of the "July effect". This is widely suspected to be as a result of the higher risk of medical errors and complications associated with the new interns beginning residency, who often do not have adequate skills and knowledge for proper patient management. Medicine is not exempt from novices, with whom there is always a margin for error, but with the human life such errors are unacceptable. Every first year resident is called an intern, and interns flood the hospitals with the intention of doing no harm as sworn with the Hippocratic oath.

I was twenty-five years old when I started residency training and had just learned to drive a manual transmission vehicle while at home in Cameroon during the month of June. This was right before returning to the U.S.A. to begin training in family medicine that July. In anticipation of training in rural Kentucky where public transportation was non-existent, learning to drive was imperative. Each day began the exact same way: first early mornings welcoming the nervous excitement that I was finally practicing medicine but will have to drive to work, and then my belly would seemingly tie up in knots, palpitations quickly followed, and my usually dry palms would become drenched in perspiration.

The first month of internship year was an inpatient medicine rotation at a busy academic center. These early mornings began with an exhaustive walk during rounds in which the senior residents' egos were palpable in speech for several hours. The day would then progress into a clerical marathon of clinical documentation that got edited multiple times before ever becoming worthy of the colossal medical record. Between getting on the road at the crack of dawn as a new international driver without a US driver's license with an ingrained fear of law enforcement versus performing competitively on the wards, I still contemplate on which daily task was most daunting. My slow, overly cautious drive back home every night ended with a sigh of relief when no one was hurt on the road or at the hospital. Thus, the end of each shift brought tremendous peace. I would recount the number of successful patient encounters and ponder on the material learned from the intensive care unit and the wards. It became a crucial daily achievement to thrive through each 24-hour segment of self-skepticism, comparison and intense but indirect competition.

With this in mind, the midway mark into my first month as an intern was worth a celebration; I had not been tagged with patients' morbidity or mortality, yet. In retrospect, my performance was comparatively good for an intern except for the fact that I was constantly fighting an impostor syndrome of feelings that I don't belong at all. These feelings were brought about by stressors in and outside of work. This was an issue I later realized several other interns struggled with in diverse ways but never mustered the courage to discuss in public. Even though times were tough, I did not foresee that things would get worse.

One evening as I arrived at my apartment I saw a piece of paper left on my door — an eviction notice. My life instantly graduated from a bit stressful at work to severely depressing both at work and now at home. This time my distress had nothing to do with being a single twenty-five year old, situational timid, lonely Cameroonian woman who worked long difficult hours for the first time in the east south-central region of the United States. I had become familiar with displacement, as there had been numerous life transitions happening every few years over the preceding eight years that all culminated to this moment in July.

Coping with work and home problems never got easier with each move. The further I got along; there was a new challenge each time which I began to expect. This time it was eviction. The shortcomings of my life in medical school had come back to me as thoughts of repeated inadequacy already during the start of intern year. In those moments I felt very alone despite having everyone around me at work. I tried to redirect my focus to what I always wanted, which was right in front of me -- a chance at a career in medicine. Yet my past flashed across my mind again as I stood there at my front door receiving such unwanted news.

Traveling from my native land Cameroon to the Caribbean for medical school and finally landing in America, my career course had been a challenging and tortuous one. It felt as if I was constantly threatened by environmental factors such as immigration, accommodation, and insufficient finances. With each of these roadblocks came a re-evaluation as to whether this career in medicine was for me. As a foreign medical student, it was frightening to urgently leave the US right after match day (the day when medical students know where they are going for residency training) to go back home to Cameroon against my wishes. My fear was centered on the low likelihood of being granted re-entry to the USA, as a denial would have truncated my career plans. My legal permission to live in America as a visitor expired seven days after match day. The law required me to return to my home country and re-apply for re-entry to the US as an alien physician/research scholar. I had suffered post-traumatic stress from four prior visa denials, and the thought of another denial right before starting residency would have stifled my dream of becoming a board-certified physician in the US. However, failure was, and remains, one thing I refuse to be acquainted with. I overcame that obstacle and now yet another one arose when I least expected it. On that fateful evening as I opened that envelope to read why I was being evicted from my subleased apartment, a feeling of despair quickly overwhelmed me. The last thing I needed, after all the struggle, in a place where I had no family within at least 500 drivable miles from me, was to be homeless.

Nineteen days prior to that moment, my father drove me to Kentucky from my official port of entry in Washington, D.C. It was the day before the start of residency orientation. Due to his own strong immigrant work ethic, he had to leave urgently the following day. I had visited Kentucky only once before, for less than 24 hours, and it was on my residency interview day. When I applied into residency, I lacked strategic mentorship causing my application process to be the opposite of meticulous. Despite good board scores, as a foreign national I only received two interview invitations.

I had lived in the US for three years prior while participating in clinical rotations as part of my Caribbean medical school's curriculum. I lived in Chicago, Illinois, doing my 3rd and 4th year rotations of medical school, and with my visa sponsorship requirement being a major limitation as a foreign medical graduate, I blindly applied to all the alien physician-friendly family medicine residency programs in the midwest and the south. I recall the hospitality I received in Kentucky in particular and how the program seemed interested in becoming a vital part of my training. I was relieved when I got the news that I matched there for residency.

Once I got to Kentucky to start residency, my father had dropped me off at this same apartment which I hurriedly secured online just to get my visa interview paperwork cleared by the American Embassy in Cameroon prior to travel. It was a furnished, two-bedroom apartment that I shared with a vibrant, Nigerian-American woman called Lola. She was a public health graduate student from Texas at the time and was exceptionally kind. I felt that she subconsciously understood the immigrant battle of being in a new environment as a Sub-Saharan African herself. We had separate leases and had never met or talked before I moved in, but that was irrelevant to me. Like other highly skilled immigrant or non-immigrant workers, my focus was on the career goals I came to achieve in the US and less about the circumstances surrounding them.

Lola's previous roommate, Anna, was my colleague from medical school. We met while doing a general surgery rotation at a dilapidated hospital on Chicago's South Side. Anna was now a second-year resident at my current 1:2 Family Medicine residency program; a training structure where learning was split between two locations. Internship (1) was primarily at a major academic center in central Kentucky, which was competitive, diverse and modern, while the 2nd and 3rd years of training were based at a rural teaching hospital in eastern Kentucky. As a result, it was usual for interns to move to the countryside at the end of first year to be within proximity to the training site. Anna had done this right before I moved in leaving me a few weeks on her lease; time enough for a sublease. As a hard-working resident herself, this was the piece of information that was omitted in our email thread prior to my travel. Our plan seemed logical and cost effective especially while making such arrangements from 4,567 miles away. After all, with a student bank account in the red, no social security number to run a background check for an apartment in my name, no credit card, and only the hope of living off my future stipend, a backdoor sublease was really all I could afford at the time. It was this or Craigslist.

After my arrival, with the anxiety of the life-changing transition in July, important personal details such as the duration of the sublease and the need to make arrangements for future accommodations were overlooked; my priority became patient care. During that entire month of July I never forgot the duration of treatment or plan of care on any of my patients' medications or orders. There weren't any therapeutic omissions associated with my name throughout that intern year. My days were filled with a cautious fretfulness about the potential for medical error. There was also a subtle dread of fulfilling a stereotype about being a lazy immigrant. As a result, I was always on time and stayed late to ensure my patients' health, safety and well being came first.

I stood outside of my apartment at sunset, less concerned about my impending homelessness and more concerned about keeping up with my performance at the hospital, adjusting to my schedule and my responsibilities for the following days. The unspoken medical culture dictates that excuses are intolerable especially from interns early in training. I resolved to dissociate from the self-torment in my thoughts and resorted to finding a quick place to stay. I was on short call the following day, which meant I got to return home late, and the last thing I wanted to do was to begin my intern year with excuses to take off my first short call. That would be defined as a "slacker move" — one that subliminally imposes that an intern can have very few personal events keep them from work in a way that increases the workload of his/her peers. I had to find a place to stay.

My first night at the cheap motel off the side of the interstate was miserable. The carpet reeked of stale petroleum mixed with mildew, a musty smell comparable to a storage room that hadn't been aerated in years. I was restless for most of the night with thoughts of possible omissions on patients I'd seen, though in actuality there were none. These thoughts coupled with the bustling sounds from trailer trucks pulling in and out from the motel garage fueled insomnia. This repeated itself each night, and I would wake up before dawn, stumble through my belongings, clean up, and leave. I nervously drove through town permit-less, arrived at the hospital to free coffee, and performed remarkably, while pretending that everything was just fine at home.

While at work, I remember purposely blocking the previous ten hours in my mind. I didn't know anyone well enough to burden him or her with my troubles. From the ethical obligations with my knowledge of medicine, I inherently knew one thing — to first do no harm to my patients irrespective of what I was experiencing. Hence, their health and safety always came first as long as I was serving as their intern doctor. *This thought pattern is common to many in training, and it is one that is paramount to the work we do. Unfortunately, the concept of self-care had not been overemphasized until the recent prevalence of the discussion around moral distress, burnout, and physician suicide within the medical community.*

I eventually settled into a stable living environment, an apartment in a newly renovated complex, with Lola again as a supportive roommate. Thankfully, I did not directly influence the incidence of the "July effect" at my facility. I also found non-pharmacological ways to combat excessive worrying and achieve balance. These included deepening my faith, creating meaningful relationships while maintaining a long distance one with my family overseas, and mindfulness based practices such as keeping a morning routine including prayer, meditation, gratitude journaling, and frequent exercise. I continue this routine till this day.

Now as a primary care physician with interest in prevention, I see how a repeated cycle of stressors brought about my improper work-life balance. Frequent displacement along with ethical and legal work obligations can become risk factors for mental health instability. I am now a proponent of evaluating environmental stressors in the lives of my patients as well as those I train as medical students or interns. With the addition of a statement on wellbeing to the Hippocratic oath, attention to our personal lives and ability will allow us to provide even higher quality care. We approach patient treatments holistically, considering socioeconomic, genetic, social and physical facets. I suggest we approach our wellbeing in the same manner. With a plan to focus my personal wellness as an early career attending, I have not yet experienced burnout in part due to the mental fortitude I built through past challenges. It took repetitive positive action, coping mechanisms, and affirmations to triumph through residency to the position of leadership as chief resident.

Reflecting on my journey pushes me to want more open discussions on the tension a career in medicine places on one's personal life, especially for women. I believe a preventative approach is best; one that identifies risks such as gender, impostor syndrome, environmental issues, frequent displacement, family obligations, system-based problems, and irrational responsibilities and creates ways to balance them out. The use of support groups within training programs and the creation of wellness initiatives as part of the curriculum for residency programs can become system based approaches to reducing the burden associated with ethical and legal obligations of medical training. Self-care can also involve a stable environment to which one can retreat to after work, muscle relaxation in a controlled environment such as massage, and other exercise-based activities as well as healthy eating education for healthcare providers, time with spouses and children, scheduled weekend vacations, and financial planning assistance during training. It took being an eager, homeless, foreign intern to develop a plan for personal self-care as a path to better patient care. I intend to continue to enhance the social stability of others who come behind me.

29

RECLAIMING MY TIME

CHARMAINE R. GREGORY, MD

This is a story of reclamation. To reclaim means to recover or retrieve something that was previously lost. As a child I had a vivid image of myself as a physician wearing a pressed long white coat and holding a shining stethoscope as I listen intently to the hearts of my patients. When I was eight years old, I would ravenously devour the high gloss vividly colored pages of the human anatomy encyclopedias my mother gave me. She knew that I had a deep desire to be just like our pediatrician. It was clear that my interest was peaked when I would repeatedly request injections on each visit to the doctor and ask an abundance of questions. This childhood dream, through the sacrifices of both my mother and myself, was realized many years after its inception.

It was this dream that sparked and stoked the flame of my mother's foresight and vision to take her only child to live in a country other than her own. The thought of how difficult it must've been for my 34 year old mother to leave behind all that she had known to emigrate to the United States with a mere $40 in her purse and two suitcases of belongings all to pursue the dream of her eight year old child gives me feelings of guilt deep inside. It was a dream that later led to sacrificing a decade of wonder and exploration, known as my 20's, in exchange for the gift of the craft that heals. The sacrifices that have been made make this reclamation story even more powerful. But how could it be that living a realized childhood dream could not bring joy? Or is it that the joy slipped away without me knowing it?

When we decide to go into medicine, our intentions are always for good. Medicine is really a craft that is predominantly pursued by those who wish to give the deepest parts of themselves to others. In fact, I did miss the parties and world traveling that my peers pursued in their twenties as I put my head down and did the things necessary to realize the dream that was born in my eight-year-old mind. So you can imagine that it was to my great surprise that I was in a position where reclamation became necessary. I had to reclaim the feelings of happiness, contentment, and resolve that danced in the heart of a eight year old child —the feelings that propelled me, this young woman, to sacrifice the exploration and frivolity of my 20's in order to learn the skills necessary to practice her dream now as an emergency medicine physician.

The altruist in me was having a difficult time reconciling with the slow creep of my loss of passion to serve and succor. How did this happen? Like every other insidious process that infiltrates and consumes, my lost love occurred over time and was an accumulation of numerous events. When you look at yourself in the mirror everyday, it is very difficult to see the metamorphosis occurring, but the change glared at me for years. I became a real life example of small daily activities having a compound effect. It was hard to see how the toll of being injured, not exercising, not finding passion outside of medicine, and not having my cup filled by medicine alone had affected me. My answer was to work more, which only worsened my depressed state and intensified the effects of burnout for me. Unfortunately, my family suffered first; I became distant and emotionally unable to accept change. This is not something that I just woke up to one day; instead, it crept upon me like a clandestine thief in the night.

The truth came out as I stood in front of a room filled with colleagues from my group's corporate office. I was faced with the reality that my journey into the abyss of burnout and the lost love for my craft had been observed by those I committed to serve. There I was discussing the balance between work and life and talking about how to incorporate meditation and other wellness activities into our busy days when one of the women in the audience shared a truth with me.

She said, "Thank you for presenting to us today. The person who stands here now is not the same person that took care of me in the Emergency Department in the fall of 2014. That person was not happy, smiling, or welcoming. She was serious, harsh and made me uncomfortable. I was relieved at change of shift when my care was turned over to your colleague for bedside rounds. I was not unhappy with the care you gave me because your plan was spot on; it was just that I felt a tension from you that was palpable. The person you are today is completely different. You are visibly happy, excited and content. I am so glad that I have been a witness to this new you."

Her words were candid and drove home the reality of my journey over the past two-year period. She was right. I was different. I am different. The night I saw her was like most in the Emergency Department, busy and chock-full of high acuity cases. I had no clue that I was coming across in the way that she described. I am indeed happy now, but I agree that I was not back then. It made me feel even more happiness when she spoke up in the group and told me what she saw. Most of all, I am grateful to have been given the opportunity to apologize to her for that night.

How did I get there? How did I fall into an enormous pit with my vision intact and not see it? What robbed my fire? Well, the answer to that question is complicated. Was it the zeal of completing training and taking on task after task in an effort to find my career niche? Was it volunteering to work shifts above and beyond my FTE (full time equivalent)? Was it not dealing with the loss of our first child or having three children in the span of four years? Was it the thought that professional mothers are expected to be excellent in everything at home, at work, and in the community? Was it solely work? Was it the combination of work, family and undue self inflicted pressures?

In January 2015, I looked in the mirror and just did not feel comfortable in my own skin as so much had changed to the point that my reflection was unrecognizable. Looking back at me was the young athlete trapped in a body that was getting older, wider, heavier and out of shape. My youngest child was 3 years old then, and I still had not been able to get out of the two clothing size upgrade that followed her birth. I was in desperate need of a change. During my pregnancy of my youngest child, I was very active with fitness classes, weight lifting, and yoga; I even ran a 5K at 27 weeks. The post-partum period with her was particularly rough though as I struggled to get back into the groove at work and regain my health. I knew something needed to be done, but it was this drive to reclaim my wellness that caused me to make some poor decisions. I ran a 5K every month during the summer season with little or no training. My body didn't tolerate the self inflicted abuse and as a consequence sustained a cryptic injury to my right knee.

This began a year long saga full of lower extremity Dopplers, an unremarkable MRI, boat loads of NSAIDs, steroid injections, numerous physical therapy sessions, several joint aspirations, a Rheumatology consultation, 50% atrophy of my right quadriceps, and loss of range of motion in my right knee. Ultimately, operative exploration was done, my knee was teeming with debris, and my meniscus was badly torn. For sure, in my mind, getting this fixed would allow my return to an active lifestyle. I tried to become more active, but I was so weak in my right lower extremity and deconditioned that my previous level of fitness was not the outcome.

I had my surgery in the summer of 2014, and I slowly started to recover both physically and mentally by January of 2015. It took all this to reveal the change that slowly occurred over the years that I did not recognize each morning as I looked in the mirror. I had to be stopped in my tracks to see that I was meeting the definition of burnout. After all, burnout is physical or mental collapse caused by overwork or stress.

As I started to workout to reclaim my fitness, not knowing what was the underlying cause for losing my joy to practice medicine, I began to feel better. The funny thing is when I started to take care of myself and consistently got an infusion of endorphins from physical exercise, all those moments that I experienced before became clear. For months I had no desire to go in at night to serve my patients. I began to recognize that I was having a hard time getting out of bed from my anchor nap when the alarm went off before work each night. The joy of my craft was gone. The enthusiasm and passion for serving, learning, and growing was gone. I looked at work as a means to pay the bills and wished constantly that I did not have to do it. The reason I had no idea I was burned out was because I did not know or recognize the signs. It was when I started to feel better that I realized how bad it actually was. The total length of my burnout is not clear to me even now. I know this; it was at least one and a half years.

I found a strategy that worked for me to stop being burned out and start taking better care of myself. Part of my reclamation of self care was documenting my fitness journey and making a concerted effort toward a positive imprint on the social space. From this fitness documentary spawned a passion to help others reclaim their fit selves. I did not know that taking care of myself would also facilitate me helping my colleagues do the same. I wanted them to experience the freedom and joy that I was able to reclaim. I dug deep into books about eating well and became very consistent with pressing play on at home workout videos. By diving into organizing fitness support groups and helping others get in shape, I discovered joy. Surprisingly, finding my inner joy brought the love back for serving my patients in the Emergency Department and the drive to embrace my craft again. It was giving back to myself that healed me. It was thinking of others that allowed me to appreciate the gift of being able to treat and serve patients night after night in our busy Emergency Department.

⚅

EVERY PERSON WHO HAS BEEN IN THE ABYSS AND RISEN OUT of it has a different narrative. The operative part of the narrative is the survival and overcoming. The path to recovery and renewal does not have to be riddled with struggle. I am very honored to now be part of a group of doctors who value their own wellness and have put in place wellness coaches, of which I am one, to help prevent burnout. Our cloth in medicine is such that breeds the attitude of resilience while we silently suffer inside, but this should not be the case. If you are a physician, resident, or medical student (or maybe you know and love one), I implore you to look critically at your heart and truly account for where you stand in terms of burnout.

How do you know if you are burned out? Do you feel fatigued, listless? Do you have anxiety when you think about going into work? Are you easily irritated or quick to anger? Have you lost your appetite? Have you been experiencing insomnia? We, as healers, serve so many, but we have to make sure that we take care of ourselves.

There is a phenomenon that tends to exclude the younger members of the house of medicine. We often attribute burnout to be a condition that is exclusive to practicing physicians who are well into their careers. This is a fallacy. The truth is you can experience the symptoms of burnout at any point in your study and training. Practicing medicine, serving patients, realizing a dream, and giving of ourselves is joyous, but there are so many things that can steal and dampen that joy. The suffocation is insidious to be sure. Forewarned is forearmed.

Even when your dream and your vision have been integral portions of your life's fabric like it was for me, the possibility of stumbling and even falling is real. It behooves us to realize that we are more resilient than we think, stronger than we know, and truly capable of amazing things. However, we all are human at the end of each day. In order to truly unleash your greatness, we have to be mindful of the external forces and often internal turmoil that can eat away slowly at our joy.

If you are in the process of this amazing journey that is the practice of medicine, please be mindful of your wellness. Your path may be very different from mine. You may find solace in journaling, sports, time with family or meditation. The key is to recognize that if your cup is not full, there is absolutely no way you can give to or serve others. It may be as simple as reading about personal development and fortification. It may be that you find the transfer of your thoughts to paper is your catharsis. Think about how you plan to practice your self-care. Give yourself 30 minutes every day just for this purpose. If you have to break this up into to 15 minute segments then so be it. There are 24 hours in everyone's day, but I implore you to reclaim your 2%.

Take your calendar out right now and pencil in your time for self-care this week. Make an appointment with yourself for yourself. Recognize if you are encroaching the abyss that is the definition of being burned out. If you are, you have a way out, you have lifelines, and you have many hands reaching down to grab yours and pull you out. Burnout is real. Burnout is indiscriminate. Burnout is sneaky. But, burnout can be defeated.

I hope that my story about the reclamation of the joy that I had lost inspires you, empowers you, and motivates you to recognize, seek help, and overcome. To serve others in this capacity as a physician is a great privilege and honor. It is our duty to ensure that we are taking care of ourselves in order to be our best. So let's preserve, claim or reclaim our joy to serve our patients. Be strong. Be brave. Unleash your greatness!

30

TO MY YOUNGER SELF

LILIANA E RIOS ROJAS, MD

What would I tell my younger self if I were able to? Well, I would start by telling her some of my experiences of how she became the physician and the woman she is today. Being born and raised in a small village of a developing country four decades ago did not place me at the best of odds to succeed in my own country, let alone in a foreign country like the US, but against all odds, I reached a level of success. How? I succeeded by always cultivating belief in myself even in some hopeless situations; the way my mother had taught me when I was a kid.

Given financial constraints, I applied to the only medical school in Colombia where tuition was income based. I took the admission test for the first time at the age of sixteen and failed three times. After failing so many times I began to doubt myself; it was the first time I failed in something scholarly related. People inside my circle of influence advised me to not pursue a career in medicine and settle where I was after having so many testing disappointments. But even when I tried to convince myself to give up on my dream, something would light up inside of me and say, "You know you are supposed to fulfill your God given destiny. So wherever in the process you might be, if you are facing opposing situations, you have to believe what you feel inside is the truth for your life; no matter what reality is showing you." Shortly after I almost gave up, fraud was discovered in the admission process for the medical school I applied to, and the test taking process was taken over by government surveillance in Colombia. I took the test a fourth time and passed.

I traveled away from my hometown to Bogota, Colombia, to start medical school. For the first two years in Bogota, I shared housing with twelve other college students and budgeted all my expenses as much as I could. I walked to campus, ate two meals instead of three when necessary (to save for books), and kept my clothing frugal (to say the least). My social life was limited to going out to my friends' and family's houses and their events. I did not belong to the most popular groups. It was something I did not give importance to at the time likely because I had a good emotional support system; two friends from college who were in different schools and a few newly developed friends in medical school with whom I am still close friends with currently.

Advice #1: Key piece of advice I can give to my younger self is to cultivate and surround yourself with people you can be yourself with and who accept you as you are. They will walk with you in life.

My Medical School Days

CLINIC YEARS STARTED, AND I MOVED TO A CONDO CLOSE to the hospital where more rotations were assigned to allow me to continue saving money on transportation. I shared the apartment with my boyfriend as well as a childhood friend.

Thankfully, I also received money from a scholarship provided by my alma mater. This gave me enough leverage on expenses so I could be more comfortable regarding buying clothing, books and meals. The trade off was that the crime rate in that area was high, but again, I relied on my support system, and my classmates and roommates created schedules to walk or travel together to and from the hospital with me.

Life in the hospital was exciting; I was finally in contact with real patients! The attendings were beyond knowledgeable. Dreaming of becoming one of them kept me going despite the hard work, hours, and shifts we had. I never saw the medical lounge and had little idea what it meant to rest.

Teaching was done at all times — even at the wee hours. I remember one particular senior resident who liked to review x-rays at 5am in order to be ready for morning rounds because he was interested in specializing in pulmonary medicine. I also remember feeling the hierarchy in place. Some seniors were mean to junior residents in front of students when they were unprepared for rounds.

"Chuky" was an internal medicine intern who was made fun of because he never seemed to be able to catch up. When his transformation took place, and he became a senior resident, he was outstanding, but sadly, he also made fun of young fellas.

Advice #2: If you are in this moment of life, keep going and studying, you will become a good senior resident for sure, even though it seems distant, you will get there. And despite hierarchy and mansplaining, mostly subtle but many times explicit, your efforts will prevail.

Experiencing Trauma

TRAUMA ROTATION WAS MY FAVORITE ROTATION OF ALL AS A

student. The hospital was a referral hospital meaning that the complicated cases were flown in from all over the country to our hospital. That, coupled with the high criminality of the area, kept cases pouring in regardless of the time of day. Cases were assigned in order of complexity by hierarchy. The most experienced took the most complicated patient cases, but usually by night cases were even assigned to the students, due to imbalance of cases verses staff. So, when I was a fourth year medical student, I was intubating, giving CPR, placing chest tubes, suturing major lacerations, and even delivered a baby when a nervous taxi driver brought a pregnant mother who was already pushing her baby out to the ER instead of taking her to the maternity hospital across the street. That day I was walking to the hospital through the ER when a nurse yelled, *"Are you a medical student?"* I nodded yes, and ten seconds later I found myself inside that car being instructed on how to deliver that baby. I do not remember the details, but I felt such a satisfaction that I was able to help her. Once the baby was delivered, the umbilical cord was clamped, and mother and her baby were transported to safety. Years later, I still think back to memories of that time to remind myself how much I am capable of doing.

I also had times in school that showed the less attractive side of medicine and people; times when I didn't feel like a rockstar student at all and experienced trauma myself. I remember doing my last anesthesia night shift with a locums anesthesiologist who was substituting for another attending. I was one of the students in the OR; it was 3am and exhaustion hit me. I requested to go to the cafeteria and grab a cup of coffee, and as I was walking through the dark hall before the corner of the small cafe, to my surprise, the attending was running behind me and asked me to wait for him so we could go together.

He started making random conversation to which I gave

short answers mainly because I was not in the mood; I was too tired to even pretend I wanted to talk. All of the sudden, he grabbed me by my hand, and pulled me towards him and tried to kiss me saying words that I don't even want to repeat. I do not know how, but I got the strength to push him over and run away.

I went to the nurse station on a different floor and from there made a phone call to my boyfriend, who came to take me home. I was upset, sad, and furious since I felt the hospital was my second home. I was so young, only 24 years old, and at the time, no one used to talk about "it". I kept quiet since I knew the following week I was moving to a different hospital, but one of the ER attendings convinced me to speak about this incident of sexual harassment. She was my cousin and promised to stick with me, but when we went together to Human Resources, somebody told her the doctor was given an unpaid vacation. It seems some events happened before, and someone had denounced him already. Although that situation was resolved, I had another instance that occurred later during my medical training.

The second event was in my intern year with a gynecology attending. He was always teaching, yet always serious-looking. One day he asked me into the medical lounge for an update on a preeclamptic young patient. Having had what happened one year earlier, I went, but I was not feeling right about it so I presented the case from the door. When I finished presenting the case, the guy stated how beautiful I was and started random conversation. He said if I wanted, I could rest there. As I started walking out, he began telling me medical orders. He did not approach me, but from that day on he persisted making subtle insinuations. Again, I felt vulnerable; I was 25 years old and far from family. I was without a support system due to the poor choice of moving to a city so far from home and friends.

Advice #3: Again, #metoo exists, and it's more frequent than thought before; it's just not openly discussed which in turn makes it invisible. But as we continue growing, and if we continue exposing these cases, we also in medicine can show that awareness has risen and zero tolerance is here.

My Decision

ONE DECISIVE EVENT IN MY LIFE WAS WHEN I HAD TO BE hospitalized with dengue fever. I had fluid around my lungs along with bleeding from my nose and in my urine. A transfusion of platelets didn't seem to help, and fever had me crippled. I overheard the attending saying somebody else had died the day before from this. I was kind of daydreaming if you will. I told myself if I survived, I would put my life on pause and travel the world for six months. I realized that I had worked so hard up to that point without allowing myself to enjoy the ride. If I was given a second chance, I was going to change my lifestyle starting with traveling.

Once I recovered, I took my passport, packed a small luggage and traveled from Colombia to the United States to visit some friends who were living there. I decided to go to Houston where one of my closest friends from high school lived. She introduced me to physicians from my country who were already doing their fellowship after finishing residency training. One month before returning home, after speaking with many of them, I made the decision to continue my journey as a physician in the US.

After practicing medicine independently in Colombia, I became a student again, now in the US, and enrolled for prep courses to take the United States Medical Licensing Examination (USMLE), a mandatory test all US doctors must take and pass. I applied for an observership where I would shadow

American doctors in order to get letters of recommendation for my application for a US residency program. Once again, I faced financial constrictions given the fact I was not able to work during those years; I used all the savings I had earned and started budgeting expenses to survive.

I repeated some of the experiences I had when I was in medical school many years before. I was confident in my abilities; my mother taught me that "self conversation" was the key. Remembering everything I had achieved up to that moment back in my country: being a homeowner, working in the ER, being able to give back to my family what I wanted, and being involved in the diabetes community through traveling the country, I gave it all up. Do not ask me why. It was not in my plans when I came here to visit, but the idea was planted in me when I spoke to my friend's best friend. He was already a researcher here and guided me on how to get started. It took me one week to deliberate with myself, and my inner voice told me. *"If you feel that you have to stay in the US, do it."* I did face the opposition in my circle of influence, but again, I decided to believe in me. It took me three years to start internal medicine residency in Lower Manhattan.

Advice #4: During those years, it took a lot of deprivation that for so many people would be almost impossible to bear, but believing in yourself, putting in the work, and having the conversation with God or whoever you believe in according to your religion, will help.

THE INTENTIONS OF MY STORIES IS TO MAKE A POINT. As women, in my opinion, we endure, and we succeed. We do not let things happen to us, we make things happen. It's on you to decide where to go. If becoming a physician is really a passion for you, there will be many joyful events to help confirm your path. New friendships await. You will form strong relationships with many patients and colleagues along the way; some you will never forget. Choose this profession if after reflection you find it can help you to conciliate your goals with your dreams in life. Take my advice; after all I went through, I am still standing.

ABOUT THE AUTHORS

AMBER ROBINS, MD, MBA

FAMILY MEDICINE

Amber Robins, MD, MBA, is a board certified family medicine doctor who is the 2017-2018 Health and Media fellow at Georgetown University School and Medicine/PBS NewsHour. She is the creator of "The Chronicles of Women in White Coats". Dr. Robins also is a medical journalist who produces patient  friendly medical resources and has written for various media outlets including PBS NewsHour, HuffingtonPost, ABC News, BlackDoctor.org, KevinMD, The Journal for Minority Medical Students in her own column entitled "Diary of a Medical Student", and 4oz Rock Magazine. She has also done on-air appearances for the national PBS NewsHour and local CBS News in Rochester, NY, discussing the latest health news.

Dr. Robins is originally from Louisiana where she attended Xavier University of Louisiana and graduated magna cum laude as a biology major and chemistry minor. She later graduated from medical school with honors in medical education and humanities from the University of Rochester School of Medicine and Dentistry in 2014. After graduating, she went to residency at Geisinger Wyoming Valley in Wilkes-Barre, PA, and later returned to the University of Rochester to complete her training in family medicine. During that time, she completed her Master's of Business Administration in 2017 from Louisiana State University-Shreveport.

Throughout her journey, Dr. Robins continues her goal of motivating others to achieve their own personal successes. Through her business, A. Robins Nest Media, she furthers her mission by coaching authors in self-publishing and through media training for health professionals.

Dr. Robins is the author of "The Write Prescription: Finding the 'Right' Spiritual Dosage to Overcome Any Obstacle" and the founder of the "Empower Now" minority professional book series. She was recently honored as the CBC/NMQF 2018 40 Under 40 Leaders in Minority Health.

Dr. Robins has her own website and blog at
www.DrAmberRobins.com.
She can also be found on twitter at @DrAmberRobins.

SURABHI BATRA, MD

PEDIATRIC HEMATOLOGY, ONCOLOGY AND
STEM CELL TRANSPLANT

Surabhi Batra, MD, is a pediatric hema-
tologist-oncologist at Robert Wood
Johnson Barnabas health system and
Newark Beth Israel Medical Center in
New Jersey. Born and brought up in
Delhi, India, she moved to the United
States of America in 2008 after completing her medical
school degree from the prestigious Maulana Azad Medical
College in Delhi, India. She pursued a residency in pediatrics
at John H. Stroger Hospital of Cook County and further
training in pediatric hematology oncology and stem cell transplantation at Ann and Robert H. Lurie Children's Hospital of
Chicago.

Surabhi is married and has two adorable boys. She has
written these stories with her life coach, her mentor, and her
best friend forever, her father, Vinod K Batra, MD, who is
also a physician, an internist practicing in India. He has been
her inspiration in every step of her life. He and Surabhi graduated from the same medical college. Talk about following

your dad's footsteps! When Surabhi decided to take this new venture in writing for this book, she could not imagine doing it without her father. He is obviously happy to be amidst 20 amazing women physicians who came together to bring you this wonderful piece of work!

MIA S. BEN, MD

PEDIATRICS

Dr. Mia Singleton Ben is a native of Napoleonville, Louisiana. She is the daughter of Joseph and Lorraine Singleton, retired educators of Assumption Parish. After graduating in 1990 from Southern University and A & M College, she then attended medical  school at Louisiana State University Medical Center in New Orleans, Louisiana, and graduated in 1995. Following medical school, Dr. Ben completed her residency in pediatrics in 1998.

Dr. Ben went on to practice pediatrics as a National Health Scholar completing her service obligation in West Alabama. In 2000, Dr. Ben started All Kids Pediatrics in Opelousas, Louisiana. After 17 years of having her own practice, she is now affiliated with Southwest Primary Health Center in Opelousas.

Along with her passion of being a doctor, Dr. Ben is also a women's professional football player, having founded the Acadiana Zydeco Women's Tackle Football Team in 2009. She is most proud that her team won a national championship in 2016. Additionally, she is also a professional baker and a talented cook.

Dr. Ben is a member of Delta Sigma Theta Sorority, Inc. She is also a Christian and a member of The Greater Ebenezer Baptist Church of Opelousas where she is a member of the deaconess ministry, medical team and is the assistant youth director.

Dr. Ben is the wife of Karl Ben, of Opelousas, and the mother of Trevon Daniel, and Mia Sofia Ben.

ALANA BIGGERS, MD, MPH

INTERNAL MEDICINE

Alana Biggers, MD, MPH, FACP, is an assistant professor of clinical medicine at the University of Illinois-Chicago (UIC), College of Medicine where she received her medical degree.

She completed residency training at the Medical College of Wisconsin in internal medicine, obtained her Master of Public Health in chronic disease epidemiology from Tulane University School of Public Health and Tropical Medicine, and completed a research fellowship at the Centers for Disease Control and Prevention (CDC).

Dr. Biggers has interests in health disparity research and achieving health equity. She has experience in breast cancer research, winning research awards while still in residency, and as a featured researcher at the National American Society of Clinical Oncology Conference and Quality Care Symposiums in 2014. Dr. Biggers continues her endeavors in research at UIC and has a NIH grant for research in diabetes and sleep. Additionally, Dr. Biggers enjoys teaching residents and medical students on best practices in urban health and providing medical care for underserved populations. She also aims to improve diversity among faculty at UIC College of Medicine as a member of both the Diversity Task Force and the Women's Task Force.

Other clinical interests include preventive health with a concentration on clinical care spotlighting lifestyle modification when providing patients with guidance. Dr. Biggers plans to expand her role in the Chicago community by providing tips on healthy living through patient care and media outlets.

ANGELA FREEHILL BROWN, MD
ORTHOPEDIC SURGERY

Dr. Angela Freehill (or Mrs. Brown at the grade school) is a woman of many hats. She is an orthopedic surgeon, a wife, a mother to three beautiful girls, a wine and cheese connoisseur, and a breast cancer survivor. She is passionate about writing and watching movies on the couch with a giant bucket of  popcorn. She loves to travel and try new places and new foods.

Dr. Freehill did her undergraduate years at Georgetown University where she completed a double major in government and psychology. She took an introduction to biology course during her senior year inspiring her to pursue medicine the summer after she graduated. She worked by day at Georgetown University Hospital as a secretary for the Department of Neurology, and went to school at night to get her pre-med requirements. She was admitted to Washington University School of Medicine in St Louis off the wait-list and subsequently moved to St. Louis, MO. She loved medical school and thrived in her third and fourth years, winning the Jesse Ternberg award as a senior which was awarded to a promising young woman entering a career in surgery.

Dr. Freehill completed her orthopedic residency at the prestigious Washington University in 2003 and then went on to do an orthopedic sports fellowship at Pennsylvania Hospital and University of Pennsylvania. She landed in Mt. Vernon, IL, after a short stint at the Marshfield Clinic in Wisconsin. She currently is on staff at Good Samaritan Hospital in Mt. Vernon, IL, and is a partner at the Orthopedic Center of Southern Illinois where she runs a general orthopedic practice with a focus on sports-related injuries and the aging knee. She just passed her orthopedic boards for the second time and is relieved not to have to do that for 10 more years.

She lives and practices in Southern Illinois with her husband, three daughters and an English bulldog named Humphrey Bogart Brown. Dr. Freehill is growing out her hair after chemotherapy and is grateful for the good hair days when they happen.

CHARMAINE R. GREGORY, MD

EMERGENCY PHYSICIAN

Charmaine R. Gregory, MD, was born in Jamaica, West Indies, and moved to New York. There she pursued her childhood dream of becoming a doctor at SUNY Buffalo School of Medicine where she earned her medical degree. After graduating, she then went to residency at Duke University Medical Center in emergency medicine. Dr. Gregory is currently a full-time nocturnist emergency physician at St. Joseph Mercy Ann Arbor Hospital in Ann Arbor, MI, where she also is an emergency medicine residency clinical faculty.

Dr. Gregory fell in love with teaching as clinical faculty but became passionate about giving others tools to reclaim wellness when ravaged by burnout. She does this through her work as an occupational wellness champion, fitness coach, and group fitness instructor. As a survivor of burnout, her recovery experience has propelled the establishment of Fervently Fit with Charmaine, LLC. Her platform is having wellness in all parts of life and discusses this through her blog, greatness coaching, and at speaking engagements.

Dr. Gregory is the wife to an entrepreneurial scientist and a mom to three vivacious cherubs. Along with her love for her family and medicine, her passion is helping busy women reclaim their wellness and unleash their greatness.

Dr. Gregory's blog can be found at:
www.ferventlyfitwithcharmaine.com/blog

PEAESHA L. HOUSTON, DO, MS

FAMILY MEDICINE

A native of Louisiana, Dr. Peaesha Houston works as a family medicine and urgent care physician serving her surrounding community. She received her bachelor's degree from Xavier University of Louisiana in biology pre-medicine with a minor in chemistry and a master's degree in biology from Georgia State University. She went on to earn a doctorate from Philadelphia  College of Osteopathic Medicine, Georgia campus. After medical school, Dr. Houston completed residency in family medicine where she served as chief resident at Gwinnett Medical Center in Lawrenceville, GA. She enjoys spending time with her family, being a mommy, and traveling.

Dr. Houston also enjoys volunteering with different organizations that support causes that are close to her heart such as adult and childhood hunger and outreach programs that aid individuals and families with financial adversities.

DANIELLE J. JOHNSON, MD

PSYCHIATRY

Dr. Danielle Johnson is a native of Erie, PA. She attended the University of Toledo for undergraduate and Drexel University College of Medicine where she graduated with her medical degree. She completed psychiatry residency and was chief resident of psychiatric emergency services at the University of Cincinnati. She has remained in the  Cincinnati area as a board certified psychiatrist. She treats adults in both inpatient and outpatient settings and particularly enjoys treating women's mental health issues such as premenstrual dysphoric disorder and perinatal mood, anxiety, and psychotic disorders.

She has served as vice president and president of the medical staff and is currently Chief of Adult Psychiatry at her hospital. She is an active member of the Ohio Psychiatric Physicians Association and a fellow of the American Psychiatric Association. Dr. Johnson is a reviewer for mental health content on UpToDate.com and womenshealth.gov and a speaker on the topics of mental health of women and minorities.

She is the mother to her 12, 19, and 20-year-old sons. The loss of their father two years ago and the resultant single parenthood is something Dr. Johnson will write about someday from a personal and professional perspective – raising strong children through grief.

Her hope is to help educate and reduce stigma about mental illness which she does through social media. Follow her on Twitter and Instagram: @drdanij

YULIA JOHNSON, DO

FAMILY MEDICINE

Yulia Johnson, DO, was born in Ukraine (former Soviet Union), where she received a degree in classical piano. She immigrated to the United States in 1992 to Denver, Colorado.

She graduated Metro State College of Denver with a Bachelor of Science in biology and chemistry and then moved to Iowa in 2001 to attend Des Moines University College of Osteopathic Medicine and Surgery where she graduated in 2005. She completed family residency at the Mercy Mayo program in Des Moines, Iowa, and was elected chief resident her senior year.

Dr. Johnson has held the job of medical director for a hospice and is an adjunct faculty at Des University College of Osteopathic Medicine. She also works at The Iowa Clinic as a family medicine physician in a rural community and lives in Des Moines, Iowa. She loves to spend her free time with her family and friends.

JULIA DRY KNARREBORG, MD

RADIOLOGY

Julia Dry Knarreborg, MD, is a native Texan and resident of Edmond, Oklahoma, currently practicing diagnostic radiology from home – the place she does her favorite and most important job as a wife and mom. She graduated fluent in Spanish and with a Bachelors of Business Administration from the University of Texas at Austin in 2001.

After witnessing the tragic events of September 11th in New York City, she began to change her career focus from business to people. A series of different jobs mixed with both personal and family struggles bridged the gap from finance to medical school, each presenting unique opportunities and challenges; together confirming even more Julia's call to medicine.

An impromptu visit to a medical school fair and her love for Spanish led Dr. Knarreborg to strongly consider Guadalajara, Mexico, for her training. Although she knew studying abroad would challenge and lengthen an already exceedingly difficult and long journey, she remained true to her heart and applied. Four months before her start date, Julia was unexpectedly faced with her biggest challenge yet — she would have to endure and complete that long journey as a single mother.

Against all odds, she graduated as valedictorian of her small class and went on to receive both Intern of the Year and Humanitarian of the Year awards during her first year of residency in New Rochelle, NY not far from the place her heart had been changed a decade earlier. She secured one of six residency spots in diagnostic radiology at the University of Oklahoma, her first choice, and was elected co-chief resident her last year of residency.

She discovered a love of writing and teaching many years ago and is excited to finally share her experiences with the world now that residency is over, and she can breathe a little. While the desire to inspire and guide others helped motivate Dr. Knarreborg's contribution to this book, more than anything, she wants her contributions to this and all future endeavors to highlight and honor God, her family, patients, Guadalajara classmates, co-residents, and all of her instructors and mentors; each of whom was instrumental in helping her achieve her dreams.

DANIELLE LOMBARDI, DDS

PEDIATRIC DENTISTRY

Dr. Danielle Lombardi (or Dr. D as her patients like to call her) strives to create only happy memories of visiting the dentist! A native New Yorker, Dr. Danielle Lombardi was born and raised in the Bronx. She earned her BA with honors in biology and psychology from Manhattanville College in Purchase,  NY. Dr. Lombardi was granted the Dean's Merit Scholarship at New York University College of Dentistry, where she earned her Doctor of Dental Surgery degree. Through her volunteer activities and patient interactions during dental school, she realized what she had always known, that she loves working with children!

Dr. Lombardi continued her education by completing a combined academic and hospital based residency in pediatric dentistry at New York University and Bellevue Hospital. During her specialty training, she received a wide range of experience working with children with craniofacial anomalies and developmental disabilities as well as medically compromised children with cancer and blood disorders. She has participated in several local and international outreach programs to Kathmandu, Nepal, Sololá, Guatemala, Machias, Maine, and Poughkeepsie, New York, to provide pediatric dental treatment, education, and training to underserved communities. She is now a diplomate of the American Board of Pediatric Dentistry.

Based on her own great experiences at the dental office as a child, Dr. Lombardi understands the importance in working individually with each patient in order to promote a lifetime of good oral and dental care. When not in the office, Dr. Danielle enjoys traveling, soul cycle, reading, and spending time with her family, friends, and bulldog Chloe.

NINA LUM, MD

FAMILY & HOSPITAL MEDICINE

Dr. Nina Lum is board-certified in family medicine and currently practices hospital medicine in Kentucky. She completed residency training at the University of Kentucky Rural Program where she graduated as chief resident in 2015. She is a health and wellness columnist, lifestyle blogger, and a health media enthusiast who also is passionate about continuing to serve on short-term medical mission trips to Africa and the Caribbean.

Dr. Lum was born and raised in Cameroon, west-central Africa, and actively helps to navigate other medical students, particularly immigrants, through careers in medicine via social media based mentorship and motivational speaking. She was a nominee for the 2018 Physician of the Year award at her institution where she currently serves as the upcoming leader of the quality department.

You can find her on the World Wide Web at
www.ninotswalk.com.

ALEXANDRA PIÑON, MD

PEDIATRICIAN

Dr. Alexandra Pinon draws from a wealth of experiences both in her professional and personal life. She moved many times as a child, and ultimately graduated from Smith College with a BA in biology. She went to the Miller School of Medicine in Miami, Florida, on the Health Professions  Scholarship Program for the United States Navy and completed her pediatrics residency at the Naval Medical Center San Diego. She served active duty in the Navy for seven years and is now a civilian working as an outpatient pediatrician in Temecula, California.

In the course of her training and career, Dr. Pinon has had the opportunity to work in the Women's Health Program at the Hospital Albert Schweitzer in Haiti; implement and participate in medical missions work in Nicaragua; and contribute to research for PEPFAR (President's Emergency Plan for AIDS Relief) in Zambia. She practiced medicine and was Chair to the Committee on Quality of Care at the Naval

Hospital in Guam. She served as an assistant professor of pediatrics while at the Naval Hospital Camp Pendleton.

Dr. Pinon strives to provide a well-rounded approach to her patients' care. She believes that creating a strong and trusting doctor-family relationship results in an enriching experience for both parties and ultimately leads to the best care outcomes for her patients. She works to support her community outside the traditional health care role having started a local chapter of the Reach Out and Read program at her office and volunteering as a Girl Scout Leader.

Dr. Pinon is a proud Navy wife and mother to her four children who are her greatest blessings.

MARIA PEREZ-JOHNSON, DO

PEDIATRIC EMERGENCY MEDICINE

Dr. Maria Perez-Johnson is a board certified pediatrician. She was born in Kingsville, Texas, and graduated from Bishop High School in Bishop, Texas (a small town with a population of around 3000). She graduated from Texas A&M University-Kingsville, with a major in biology and a minor in chemistry. She  joined the Ronald E. McNair Scholars program as an undergraduate student and conducted research at the National Natural Toxins Research Center. Her undergraduate research involved isolating proteins from snake venom for potential biomedical applications. She also did a summer internship at Texas A&M University - College Station where she isolated proteins from fungi in order to develop specific isolate proteins that would aid in other biomedical applications.

She graduated magna cum laude in 1997 and following graduation began her studies at the University of Health Science Center, Texas College of Osteopathic Medicine in Fort Worth, Texas. She completed her pediatric residency at

Texas A&M University, Driscoll Children's Hospital. She is board certified in pediatrics and has practiced pediatric emergency medicine at Driscoll Children's Hospital, Edinburg Children's Hospital, Children's Hospital of San Antonio, Dayton Children's Hospital in Ohio, and Sunrise Children's Hospital in Las Vegas, Nevada. She has served as the pediatric department chair at Driscoll Children's Hospital as well as worked on numerous committees at various institutions to focus on the health of the children of South Texas. She has been a pediatric faculty member at the University of Texas Medical Branch at Galveston, Texas, A&M University Medical School and is currently teaching faculty at Baylor College of Medicine through the pediatric residency program at Children's Hospital in Santa Rosa.

Dr. Perez-Johnson has been happily married for over 30 years and has two adult children. She spends her free time traveling with her family and taking walks with her bulldog, Zeus.

LILIANA E RIOS ROJAS, MD

NEPHROLOGY

Dr. Liliana Rios is a nephrologist in the state of Texas. Born and raised in Colombia, South America, Dr. Rios graduated from the National University of Colombia as a physician specializing in general surgery. She worked a few years in her home country, mainly in the emergency room and hospitalist areas. She also managed an outpatient  program for patients with diabetes and hypertension in her home city.

Dr. Rios was also able to impact the lifestyle of a large group of patients in a unique multi-disciplinary program. In this program, patients were able to be evaluated and supported in their health journeys with a range of resources from having a nutritionist to a psychologist, and once in a while, were even able to have an exercise session with physical therapy along with their physicians all in one group.

After practicing medicine in Colombia, Dr. Rios moved to the United States later in her career where she pursued internal medicine. She completed her internship at New York Downtown Hospital and later finished her training in the areas of internal medicine, geriatrics and nephrology at Winthrop University Hospital in Long Island.

Dr. Rios currently works in a private practice group in the state of Texas where she lives with her family who includes her three year old daughter, Valerie. Dr. Rios is keen to empower other women around the country to change their lives and convey to their future what they were born to do. Her goal is also to promote a better future for her own daughter and so many others.

ARCHANA R. SHRESTHA, MD

EMERGENCY MEDICINE

Archana Reddy Shrestha, MD, MS, FACEP, is a board-certified emergency medicine physician who practices in Chicago. She obtained her medical degree at the University of Illinois at Chicago in 2004 and completed emergency medicine residency at George Washington University in 2008. She is also an associate professor with the  Chicago Medical School at Rosalind Franklin University of Medicine and Science.

In addition, Archana holds a Masters in Journalism from the University of Illinois at Champaign-Urbana. Her writing has been published by the Chicago Sun Times, KevinMD, and ABC News. She has also been a national spokesperson for the American College of Emergency Physicians for over a decade. In 2008, she had the unique opportunity to be the doctor on set for the filming of the James Bond movie "007: Quantum of Solace."

As a medical student, she was awarded a prestigious

Fulbright Fellowship for the study of medical anthropology in Ecuador where she observed traditional Ecuadorian healers and catalogued their medicinal plants.

Archana was recently named one of the Top 20 Global Women of Excellence by U.S. Congressman Danny K. Davis in recognition of her achievements not only in medicine but also as an online fitness and nutrition coach who empowers busy working moms to achieve health and wellness.

Her healthy living lifestyle blog can be found at MightyMomMD.com.

KENDRA SEGURA, MD

OBSTETRICS/GYNECOLOGY

Kendra Segura, MD, MPH, FACOG, is an obstetrician-gynecologist who is known as Dr. Kendra: Your Ob/Gyn Next Door®. She currently works at Kaiser Permanente in southern California. A native of Los Angeles, California, she attended Ross University School of Medicine, and completed her residency training at Rochester Regional Medical Center in Rochester, New York. She also has a Masters of Public Health from Loma Linda University, in Southern California.

Dr. Segura's unlimited passion for women's health extends beyond the walls of the hospital, and she is always looking to reach out to women using any means possible. People will find relevant, current, inspiring, and often amusing information shared by Dr. Segura in various formats and on different platforms, including Instagram. She has authored and been involved in articles, videos, and podcasts for public awareness. She is also a permanent fixture at LaughingSarah.org, an organization whose mission is to support women and couples dealing with infertility.

Dr. Segura's emphasis on prevention and public education started before she even entered medicine when she was working as an epidemiologist for the Los Angeles County Department of Public Health. It was there she realized the importance of public education and the public's health. Dr. Segura believes it is her God-given purpose to inform the uninformed and misinformed. In so doing, she hopes to empower women to take care of their own health.

By dispensing the medicine of knowledge, Dr. Segura aims to help all women, even those that are not a part of her practice. She also seeks to empower women by sharing stories of struggles and success, not just of her own, but the many inspirational women that she feels fortunate in meeting. She hopes that all women will be able to realize their own true worth and continue aspiring. With so many women to help, her job is never finished, and Dr. Segura will continue to work tirelessly to keep women happy, healthy and inspired.

KENA SHAH, DO

ADULT & PEDIATRIC ALLERGY & IMMUNOLOGY

Dr. Kena Shah is a board-certified physician dually accredited in allergy & immunology as well as internal medicine. She completed her undergraduate degree in biology with a pre-medical concentration from University of North Carolina at Charlotte. While she was getting her undergraduate degree, she  was commended to the Dean's list and graduated with university honors. She was also recognized in Beta Beta Beta, a national biological honors society.

Dr. Shah then attended medical school at Philadelphia College of Osteopathic Medicine in Atlanta, GA, where she was recognized as a member of Sigma Sigma Phi, an honorary fraternity. She then did her internal medicine residency at University of Medicine and Dentistry of New Jersey/Jefferson Health System of New Jersey. Dr. Shah received her adult and pediatric training in allergy, asthma, & immunology from Nova Southeastern University located in Florida. During her fellowship, she was honored as a Chief Fellow.

Dr. Shah has been actively involved in research since her undergraduate days. She won a national prize for a case presentation at the American College of Osteopathic Internists. Dr. Shah has presented at many national conferences and is a corresponding author of a book. Dr. Shah has had many publications over the years in the field of Allergy and Immunology.

In her free time, Dr. Shah enjoys spending time with her family and doing outdoor activities. In the future, she wishes to join a non-profit organization to help underprivileged kids. Dr. Shah wishes to touch the world by encouraging people to follow their dreams, be fearless, and speak up for their values.

NATASHA K. SRIRAMAN, MD, MPH

PEDIATRICS

Natasha K. Sriraman, MD, MPH, FAAP, FABM, completed her education and training in Pennsylvania and New York. Prior to getting her MD, she attained her MPH in health policy and maternal/child health.

Currently, Dr. Sriraman works at The Children's Hospital of the King's Daughters/Eastern Virginia Medical School (CHKD/EVMS) in Norfolk, Virginia, as an associate professor of pediatrics. She has published on the topics of breastfeeding, postpartum depression, public health in pediatrics, and oral health. She has served on the board of the American Academy of Pediatrics (AAP)-Section of Breastfeeding, Virginia Chapter of the AAP, and Postpartum Support Virginia. She is currently a board member of the Academy of the Breastfeeding Medicine and also serves on the board of FOR KIDS homeless shelter in Norfolk, Virginia.

Dr. Sriraman served as a strategic team member for www.BFConsortium.com, writing modules for Maintenance of Certification Parts 2 and 4. She has designed resident curriculums in both breastfeeding and public health for CHKD. She is also on the executive committee for the Women in Medicine and Science at Eastern Virginia Medical School.

She speaks Spanish and Hindi and uses her experiences when addressing cultural competency topics within her practice, teaching, lectures, and research.

Dr. Sriraman is passionate about legislative advocacy and has traveled to Washington, DC, and Richmond, VA, to lobby about various child health issues. She worked with the Virginia-AAP Chapter and governor to have May declared as Maternal Mental Health Month in the state of Virginia.

Dr. Sriraman is an avid runner and loves hot yoga, kickboxing, and barre. She has run multiple half marathons, a marathon, and a 50K (her first and last!) She lives in Virginia Beach with her husband, three children, and her doubledoodle puppy.

BANDE VIRGIL, MD

PEDIATRIC HOSPITALIST

Dr. Bande Virgil is an author with publications and interviews on several well known websites including The Bump, Romper, and KevinMD. She also writes regularly on her own blog 'The Mommy Doc' where she shares the journey of motherhood and gives practical advice on children's health and parenting.

Dr. Virgil is a dedicated wife and mother to two young children who have given her insight into the challenges of balancing family life and world expectations as a parent. She is passionate about motherhood: affirming mothers of all backgrounds in their journey to raise healthy children and reclaim the fun of parenting. Without solid family networks our children cannot reach their fullest potential.

She is also passionate about the practice of medicine. She believes in empowering and training students and residents to practice medicine with excellence and compassion for their patients as well as their colleagues.

Dr. Virgil is a board certified pediatrician and clinical assistant professor of pediatrics who has worked both in private practice as well as in the hospital.

You can follow her on facebook at "The Mommy Doc"; on instagram @themommydoc1; or www.themommydoc.com. Her parenting advice book , A Teaspoon of Honey: New Millennium Parenting will be available in 2018.

LATASHA SELIBY PERKINS, MD

FAMILY MEDICINE

Dr. LaTasha S. Perkins is currently a college health physician at Georgetown's Student Health Center, an assistant professor in the School of Medicine, and immediate past medical editor of Heart & Soul magazine.

Her accomplishments include the 2017-2018 chair and delegate for the American Academy of Family Physicians (AAFP) Membership Constituency, AAFP NCCL Women's Co-Convener 2017, Congressional Black Caucus (CBC) Annual Legislative Conference panelist, Congressional Tri-Caucus Minority Health Disparities Summit speaker, 2015 Society of Teachers of Family Medicine New Faculty Scholar and the CBC/NMQF 2016 40 Under 40 Leaders in Minority Health Honoree.

She recently became a young professional member of the National Minority Quality Forum Advisory Board and was featured on Upworthy.com for her advocacy and work in preventive medicine. Dr. Perkins' hope is to aggressively influence positive change in health care disparities, health education of underserved populations, and mentorship to impact success rates of diverse students in medicine and STEAM.

KAREN WILLIAMS

EDITOR, "THE CHRONICLES OF WOMEN IN WHITE COATS"

Karen Williams was raised in Baton Rouge, Louisiana; she is a Louisiana girl and is proud of it. Her parents raised their four children in a small neighborhood filled with many other loving families during the 60's and 70's. Her father was a hard-working man who made it possible for her mother to stay  home and raise the children. The kids were blessed to attend a local Catholic school which instilled the love of God and a the strong faith that built the family many generations ago. Her parents were especially active at their school where her daddy was a football coach and the medicine man for the local Indian Guide chapter, and her mamma was a Girl Scout leader and a cafeteria volunteer every Monday.

Karen grew up in Girl Scouts and spent her summers through college working at Camp Marydale in St. Francisville, Louisiana. It was through spending summers with the girls that she developed her love for working with children and decided to major in Elementary Education at Southeastern Louisiana University. After graduating in 1986, she began her 25 year career as a classroom teacher in the Diocese of Baton Rouge Catholic School System. It was through her teaching that she was introduced to The Shurley Method (www.theshurleymethod.com); at the time it was a new innovative way to teach writing and grammar. English grammar became her passion; teaching it became even more exciting through this method. When the students became excited about it, that was all she needed to encourage her to teach as much grammar and writing as she could. It was through these years of teaching English grammar and writing and editing 40-60 research papers twice a year that she became interested in editing.

Throughout her life she also has been able to incorporate her love for music that began when she was a young child. In each of her schools where she worked she was asked to lead the children in singing with her guitar at weekly student masses and also sang and played guitar in her parish choir for many years. She always felt closest to God through singing whether it was with the children or in church.

Even though she is no longer in the classroom, she keeps her love of educating alive by tutoring as many students as possible and teaching anyone who wants to learn how to crochet. She even has an Etsy shop online, KarensCuteCreations, where she sells her crochet creations. When Dr. Amber Robins, a former student, approached her to begin editing for Amber Robins' Nest, it was like God was opening yet another door for her. It was a way for her to continue using her skills in English grammar.

Karen is blessed to remain very close to her siblings as well as their children and grandchildren. She now lives in Denham Springs, Louisiana, with her sister and brother-in-law in a home she and her family built themselves. She loves to go camping and spends as much time with her family as possible. God is good.

REFERENCES

1. "Professionally Active Physicians by Gender." *The Henry J. Kaiser Family Foundation*, 26 Jan. 2018, www.kff.org/other/state-indicator/physicians-by-gender/?currentTimeframe=0&sort-Model=%7B%22colId%22%3A%22Location%22%2C%22-sort%22%3A%22asc%22%7D.

2. Greenfield, R. (2017, April 27). Women Doctors Earn Less-and Not Because of the Jobs They Choose. Retrieved April 14, 2018, from https://www.bloomberg.com/news/articles/2017-04-27/women-doctors-earn-less-and-not-because-of-the-jobs-they-choose

3. More Women Than Men Enrolled in U.S. Medical Schools in 2017. (2017, December 18). Retrieved April 14, 2018, from https://news.aamc.org/press-releases/article/applicant-enrollment-2017/

4. Data and Reports - Workforce - Data and Analysis - AAMC. (n.d.). Retrieved April 14, 2018, from https://www.aamc.org/data/workforce/reports/458712/1-3-chart.html

5. Tsugawa, Y., Jena, A. B., Figueroa, J. F., Orav, E. J., Blumenthal, D. M., & Jha, A. K. (2017). Comparison of Hospital

Mortality and Readmission Rates for Medicare Patients Treated by Male vs Female Physicians. *JAMA Internal Medicine*, *177*(2), 206–213.
http://doi.org/10.1001/jamainternmed.2016.7875
6. Section II: Current Status of the U.S. Physician Workforce. (n.d.). Retrieved April 14, 2018, from
http://aamcdiversityfactsandfigures.org/section-ii-current-status-of-us-physician-workforce/#ref1
7. Data-Driven Diversity and Inclusion Change. (n.d.). Retrieved April 14, 2018, from
http://aamcdiversityfactsandfigures2016.org/report-section/section-2/
8. By the numbers: Women in the U.S. military. (2013, January 24). Retrieved April 14, 2018, from
https://www.cnn.com/2013/01/24/us/military-women-glance/index.html
9. Stith AY, Nelson AR. Institute of Medicine. Committee on Understanding and Eliminating Racial and Ethnic Disparities in Health Care, Board on Health Policy, Institute of Medicine. Washington, DC: National Academy Press; 2002. Unequal Treatment: Confronting Racial and Ethnic Disparities in Health Care.
10. Physician Suicide. (2017, June 12). Retrieved April 14, 2018, from https://emedicine.medscape.com/article/806779-overview